*Du... ur teful with Blessings + Love*

*Let heart. Patricia*

# Accepting Death, Embracing Life:
## How Death Teaches Us to Live

# Accepting Death, Embracing Life:

# How Death Teaches Us to Live

Patricia Gulino Lansky

Land and Sky Publishing
Charlottesville, Virginia

www.PatriciaGulinoLansky.com

ISBN-13: 9781517722173
ISBN-10: 1517722179
Library of Congress Control Number: 2015916770
CreateSpace Independent Publishing Platform
North Charleston, South Carolina

# DEDICATION

I dedicate this book to my parents, Anna Marie and Leonard A. Gulino, who lovingly chose to give me the great gift of life. I am blessed by their commitment to manifesting an ever expanded existence. And to all who share love and compassion with me. You fill my life with grace and I am eternally grateful.

# HEAVEN ON EARTH

Cradled in the dangling tree house
of an implausible air balloon
I am gliding silently
one hundred feet off the ground
inhaling intoxicating pine
reaching down to bestow blessings
on each tree top, pinecone,
all fearless birds flying high.

Ethereal breeze carries me.
I witness the valley and hills below
Japanese landscape
deep forest in the mists,
wishing I could stay suspended forever.

Farms and farmer, sheep, chickens and cattle
pieces from a manger
so detailed,
so dear.
Oh Life, I want to embrace you closer!

What keeps me suspended?
No ropes or pulleys,
only fire and air.
Like fire in my heart,
inhaling cool breezes
exhaling warmed moist air.

# Accepting Death, Embracing Life

Invisible energy holds me afloat
drifting on wings of wind
until I land
feather to earth.

This ride is over
yet its resonant beauty
remains in my soul,
and in all I have touched.

# Contents

# Preface

EVERY SOUL HAS a unique and divine purpose to accomplish during its time here on earth. Some souls demonstrate their purpose by example and inspire through their stories, struggles and triumphs. And there are other equally courageous souls who show by example the road to avoid, lest you descend, as they did, into your own parallel hell.

I was privileged to know a remarkable soul who must have agreed in the spirit realm to be born into this world to live a life of limitation and suffering in order for her life to become an unmistakable wake up call to anyone who would listen.

My friend died in a difficult, frightened and painful way.

Her medical journey began with her doctor not hearing her, ignoring her words that she was in pain. Months later he saw test results and admitted she had been telling him the truth.

In April, she began treatment and made progress with surgery and chemotherapy. In July, the doctor reported that all four tumor sites were shrinking and that she and her husband should plan a celebration vacation by Christmas after the completion of treatments eradicating the cancer. But in September, everything stopped working. She complained of great pain in her side. By October, after a week of observation, tests and pain medication trials, the doctor announced that my friend had a tumor filling her stomach past its walls which had created such a complete blockage that there was nothing more they could do for her.

Shock waves went shivering through all who knew her. Questions emerged. How did her doctors miss this enormous blockage that wouldn't allow her to ingest anything ever again, other than sips of water and teaspoons of crushed ice? For the next three and a half weeks she sat and waited for death to take her. Why couldn't they find the right pain medication combination to make her comfortable? Even thirty-six hours before she died, she was still sitting up in a wheel chair with no head rest, with swollen feet and no foot rest, barely able to speak, holding her side as she cried in a small voice, "Please somebody help me…"

Why was she so afraid to die?
Why was she unsure of what to expect in the dying process?
Why was she flooded by regrets and unfinished business?
Why did she fear God's wrath?
Was there anything that could have helped her to have a more peaceful process of dying?

You hold in your hands my answer to my friend's cry. This book is my attempt to help all of us turn our fear of our own death and the grief of losing our loved ones into peace and freedom. Within these pages may you find tools to expand your experience of self-discovery and self-transformation as you examine your own thoughts, feelings and questions about death <u>and</u> life.

# Introduction

"TODAY IS A good day to die."

Perhaps you've heard this phrase in old Westerns spoken by Native Americans, or by the Klingons in the television show "Star Trek: Next Generation," declaring the same. Could you ever imagine this would be something you would say? One ordinary day, quite by chance, while encountering a typically noisy and grimy street on New York's Upper West Side, everything aligned in me in such a way that I said exactly that, "Today is a good day to die."

Don't get me wrong. I had no wish to die. I love life. I love the beauty of the earth and the people and all the world's variety. If I got the chance, I would certainly sign up for a return engagement on earth in a future life.

I made the "good day" statement just before my thirtieth birthday. A year earlier on my twenty-ninth birthday, I felt like I was going to die. I wasn't at all ill. I just felt that I wouldn't make it through another year. These thoughts filled me with terror.

Just prior to this special day, I came to a significant resolution about my father's death, my dear father, who I lost when I was fifteen. The formerly abstract concept of death became a heavy reality, like a boulder in the middle of my teenage years. I would never be the same again. Beginning with my father's death until my mother's death twenty-two and a half years later, I experienced seven deaths of family members—about one every three years. All were from long term illnesses. Doctors, diagnoses, hospitals, treatments and death became a way of life, schooling me in the realities of end of life.

So on that ordinary day, on a street filled with busy people, a revelation, a moment of grace embraced me. In that moment, with no outward change in me, I had an epiphany because of the emotional work I'd been doing to resolve my father's death. The day before, in a group process, I witnessed a friend of mine express her feelings about the loss of her father whom she deeply loved. Through the process of witnessing and empathizing with my friend's grief, I found the internal permission to clarify my confused emotions at the loss of my own father. My new awareness that emerged from finding my emotional truth, freed me to fully experience the beauty of life in that moment on that street in New York City. I knew that if I died right then—all would be okay. I would have no remorse, no regrets, no fear. I felt full, resolved, so at one with all that is, that I knew "Today is a good day to die." And because of that full allowing, it was also a good day to live.

And then the world shone with a beauty and light that glistened, even on that dirty pavement. I fell in love with all that I could see. I accepted my feelings about the loss of my father and I felt for the first time, free of the confusion and guilt about my thoughts and feelings. It was as if I'd been drowning in the ocean and finally broke through the surface and tasted the fresh air. It was the beginning of my process of coming to understand who I am and what the spiritual reality is for each one of us. In this moment of grace, I became aware of a greater, freer life available to me. It was the beginning of transcending my fear and despair surrounding death and learning about the many resources to deal with dying and living.

My desire to write this book is to accompany those of you who are now or will be witnessing the dying process and death of someone you love. The book is also designed to prepare all of us for our own inevitable death. This work of acceptance will empower us to embrace our one precious life more fully than ever before.

As a psychotherapist since 1984 and an ordained minister since 2001, I have connected with countless individuals in their time of transition from life to death. My writing is my response to the need in me and the need I see in many people who deeply wish to have some guidance and direction during one of the most difficult passages we might ever witness or experience ourselves. It is my way of being present with you as you read.

Although I am a minister, and I do have a personal connection with the God of my understanding, it is not my purpose to convert anyone to a particular religious orientation. Whether you believe in a Higher Power or not, this book is still for you. Even though this is not a religious book, I do quote from many world religions and from other sources where I find wisdom. This universal wisdom about death and life can be found in all times and on all spiritual paths. We can be supported by those who have gone before us and have grappled with these same issues.

During the time I was writing this book I realized I needed to discover the final piece of how to hold the whole issue of death and dying. I had only begun to write when I started to get physically sick. Dwelling on death and memories of sadness surfaced in laryngitis. I grieved every memory anew, experiencing it as if for the first time. I wondered how I could possibly proceed when the writing hurt so much.

When I lost my voice, I realized in a new way that creation is voice. I knew I had to create a new voice, a new way to express all of this, in order to survive writing about it. As a result, I developed a way of healing my relationship with death. This method is divided into seven chapters or seven phases. In each phase you will find personal examples. Think of these phases not in a linear way. You don't have to heal this first and then that. The process is a spiral of growing understanding happening simultaneously. Feel free to choose whichever phase calls to you at a given time. Eventually, integration of all phases will be required to complete your healing.

At the end of each chapter there is a "Sacred Process" section containing questions and activities for reflection, discussion, journaling, and further development of each of the seven phases necessary to accept death and embrace life. There are no right answers. The questions are simply suggestions to encourage you to explore more deeply. If you find that you wish you had more help in this process, please seek a counselor or support group.

**Chapter 1: Cultural Programing**—covers the mundane, earthly view of death including the confusion and denial surrounding aging and mortality, and the avoidance of the subject of death and dying.

**Chapter 2: Befriending Your Feelings**—focuses on the importance of feelings and expressing your emotions about death, especially the "difficult" emotions like anger and grief are included and discussed.

**Chapter 3: The Soul Revealed**—speaks about what I believe actually happens to us as immortal souls when we die.

**Chapter 4: Expanding Our Thinking**—explores the thoughts and beliefs that we have consciously and unconsciously attached to death. You will uncover your beliefs and find ways to change the beliefs that no longer work for you.

**Chapter 5: My Journal**—moves you through the personal experience of a terminal illness and death of a loved one.

**Chapter 6: The Heavens Open**—describes the dying process and the mystical openings that are often present at the time of death.

**Chapter 7: Developing a Practice of Letting Go**—encourage the development of the powerful practice of letting go and surrendering to life in all its manifestations.

I invite you to walk with me through my experiences so that I can be next to you during your time of need. Each death is so completely individual, yet I believe our experiences have more in common than we might imagine. As we open our conversation around death and dying I will be by your side guiding, not leading you. Learn from my experiences what you can, and know you are not alone.

My intention is that by reading this book, your journey will be a little lighter and you will come to no longer fear death. Free of fear, you will see that death is naturally a part of life, and in that acceptance, you will discover not only what it means to live fully until you die, but you will also become a bridge for your loved ones so that they may peacefully, gently, and with dignity embrace the great and mysterious adventure that we call death.

As you read this book and come to terms with death and dying, may you come to understand that you are an eternal soul, so that transformation of consciousness will emerge from within you. The opportunity is here for you to awaken to the Truth of who you really are.

# CHAPTER 1

## Cultural Programing

"In all manners of life, be informed by death."

— CARLOS CASTANEDA

## A Home of Our Own

THE DESIRE OF the heart is a double-edged sword. It cuts to the core of what you yearn for, focusing you on attaining that cherished dream while demanding a cutting away of the old and worn. So this desire can become a vehicle for growth and transformation.

My mother and father's desire to own their own home propelled us most Sunday afternoons for years on a pilgrimage to find our dream house. We were all being schooled in the fine art of house hunting. We'd pile into the car, parents, brothers and me, with the promise of a new listing. Off we'd go on an adventure to canvas the city for possibilities, always to no avail. The potential house always came down to a split decision between my parents.

Eventually, when I was eleven, certainly old enough to have an opinion, I broke the stalemate. Dad and I voiced a two to one decision and although not a firm yes from Mom, she decided to side with us. We got our own home, my parent's first and only home, on Anderson Place. That home became the container of our lives and deaths for the next twenty-five years: the exact length of the mortgage.

Our new home was a turn of the century Victorian jewel with two large porches front and back, solid hardwood floors, wainscoting on the walls and pocket doors between the dining room and double living room, a fireplace, and my favorite lead glass bay windows that made prisms of the sunlight. To me, the house was beautiful.

My parents had the option of taking insurance that would pay off the entire mortgage if either one of them should die before the mortgage was paid in full. The insurance was an added expense, of course, and since they were young and healthy, they chose to refuse the added insurance. Six months later, my Dad was diagnosed with cancer.

I know he deeply regretted not being able to save us from that financial burden. He berated himself that he would not now be able to give us this substantial gift at the time of his death. I observed sadly how this decision weighed heavily on him.

Death moved into our newly purchased home in July, when I was just fifteen years old. Once death moves in, it never leaves. It weaves itself into the bones of the home and right into the DNA of the souls who live there. My early years contained lessons that I never would have chosen to receive, but have made me who I am, have molded my very soul with an indelible stamp.

My life started off as usual as any. With the death of my pet parakeet, my parents helped me to understand that all living things die. We even had a burial of my dear pet. He had charmed us all by learning to speak from an instructional record and say his name with such pride, "Pretty Boy Bobbie."

My parents didn't try to shelter me from the facts of life. I was allowed to see my Grandmother in her casket when I was six years old. But it was the death of my father, and the events leading up to his death, for which I was most unprepared.

Living in our beautiful Victorian house in Buffalo, New York where my father died, began a journey for me that has taken me to places of the heart I never knew existed. And so many years later, another Victorian house, in Bath, Maine, the setting of my mother-in-law's death, has taken me full circle. Whereas once I feared death, now I accept it.

### "Oh My Papa"
"Oh my Papa, to me he was so wonderful,
Deep in my heart, I miss him so today."
Parsons, Turner, Burkhard

At three years old I recorded this popular song, "Oh My Papa," on a record that was made with the then modern equipment at a dance studio where I took ballet and tap lessons. My Mom jumped on the studio's idea to make this record as a surprise for my Daddy for Father's Day. I remember how serious I was singing this song that I learned from Mommy. I was precariously perched on a box that allowed my mouth to be level with the large microphone at the top of a pole. When I finished the song, Mom chuckled. She didn't know that her glee was captured on the recording. There was a skip on the record right in the middle of her laugh; so her sound repeated in an odd rhythm which always made all of us laugh along with her whenever we heard the recording.

When I gave the record to my Daddy on Father's Day, I remember him holding me in his arms in his favorite deep red comfy chair. Mom placed the record on the Victrola and was right by our side as we listened together. Among hugs and kisses and elation, I knew I was the center of a world of affection and appreciation, cared for and seen by these parents I adored. But with the loss of Dad, there were so many haunting questions I never had the chance to ask him.

I have memories that confirm my understanding of who my father was. Leonard Gulino, was a brilliant self-made man who developed a thriving practice as a barber in an exclusive society men's club. He was busy six days a week and was very well liked by all the people with whom he came in contact. He was a refined and elegant man. I once asked him if he talked to the clients or kept quiet when he was cutting their hair. He wisely told me he just responded to the cues they gave him about what they preferred. It was about serving them, not his own agenda.

My Dad's kindness and generosity were abundantly present. On Sunday, his one day off each week, we would often visit our cousins and Dad would bring his tool kit and spend much of his afternoon cutting the three boys' hair. Dad often cooked on Sundays to give Mom the day off. Although Mom was a fabulous cook, I never tasted a tomato sauce as rich and filled with layers of flavor as his.

Mom told me stories of Dad encouraging her and Grandma to attend midnight Mass on Christmas Eve while he agreed to finish putting up the tree and all the trimmings. Mom and Dad wanted to make Christmas morning magical for us, as if Santa brought everything during the night, just like the story said. When she came home, she found him exhausted and sound asleep under the tree, with all the lights on, surrounded by parts of the new toys he was assembling for us.

Dad loved to bowl and received many trophies for bowling three hundred point perfect games in the leagues as well as in national competitions. He always served as the anchor man on teams. This is the person who bowls last and is expected to come through for the team and make up the point difference if needed. Of course this can place a lot of pressure on that person, but Dad had such an even disposition and an inner calm that he was never riled and consistently championed his teams to success.

As a kid, I was amazed at the depth of Dad's composure when I watched helplessly as one of my cousins, just a kid himself, rolled a heavy cart down his driveway and accidentally hit my Dad's leg with great force. I could see Dad wince in pain, unable to walk for a bit. Yet he never struck back or castigated my cousin. I'm sure he understood my cousin didn't mean to harm him.

I am glad for these and other memories of my father and yet I felt robbed of more that I might have known about him if we'd had more conversations in our family. Unfortunately, regret can play a large part in our grief when we lose a loved one.

When I was about thirteen, I could see that Dad was not feeling well at times but I didn't know the reason and no one told me what was wrong with my Dad. One summer day, while he was driving me to one of my many extracurricular activities with friends, Dad suddenly pulled the car to the side of the road. He just made it there when he had to lie down on the seat. He couldn't move or talk for what seemed like a long time. I had the car door open and people started to gather on the sidewalk gawking at my poor Dad. I was frightened and protectively told them to stop staring and go away. Some listened.

Of course, I was aware that at every meal Dad was having a lot of trouble swallowing food because of the radiation treatments he received on his throat and naso-pharynx. We didn't talk about why he was having those treatments. Eventually, we bought a blender, and Mom liquefied his meat, potatoes, and vegetables into an awful-colored glop. He would spend hours at the kitchen table, well after we were all done and the dishes were washed and put away, trying to ingest some of his food. He said none of it had any taste. His taste buds must've been burnt out from those treatments that also removed some of his hair and burnt the skin on his neck, making it look like dried-out, tanned leather.

We took a family trip to Philadelphia to visit Dad's older brother, Uncle Joe. It was wonderful seeing Uncle Joe again so when we returned home and I saw a letter from him, I opened it with excitement. I told my parents I had done so and they asked me to read the letter out loud. Uncle Joe said that Dad should have hope for a cure because there are successful treatments for cancer these days. Completely astonished I said, "Does Dad have cancer?"

"Yes," was the answer. That was the beginning and end of our discussion. I got the clear message not to talk about this subject ever again, so I didn't.

In my mind I always felt Dad would recover and heal. At fifteen years old, I couldn't imagine anything else. I know now that my parents were trying to protect me. I don't blame them. Talking about death, especially with children wasn't a common practice in our death-denying culture. At that time, there were few models of how to be open and honest about death. The movie, *Terms of Endearment*, in 1983, reflected the change beginning to occur in our society's practice of avoiding speaking about death. The movie showed a mother having a conversation with her children, explaining to them that she was dying. We, unfortunately, never had that conversation.

I had just completed my freshman year of high school and had decided to take biology with my best friend, Carm, during the summer. Our lab work required us to dissect a frog. I understand this practice has been removed from biology labs in some schools. How lucky for the frogs and for the students. We worked in pairs and gratefully, Carm did the cutting. I still remember the smell of formaldehyde and frog, the nauseating experience of a pinned and splayed animal and a chemical of numbing deadness. I felt this was not a course in which I could excel. I had seen enough medical experiments done on my father. I sensed the irony of learning biology, the study of life, through a dead creature.

Then July 8 came, a bright and sunny summer day. It was the kind of day we Buffalonians wait for all year. It was a day to escape to the beach or pool and don our bathing suits to be free and easy and refreshed by the sun and water and carefree movement. My cousin Connie invited me to go swimming at a new, large pool. My Mom encouraged me to go. She would spend the day with Dad in the hospital and planned to stay overnight again as she had done several times in the past two weeks. She asked me to come the next morning around nine a.m. to relieve her.

The day before, Dad had an emergency tracheotomy because he couldn't breathe. His air passage was cut off because of the accumulation of scar tissue from radiation on his neck. So they sliced a hole in the front of his throat, like we had sliced that frog. He could breathe again, but he couldn't speak. They assured us, in time, he could learn to speak again through his voice box, creating a type of burp that could be amplified by a sounding mechanism. But for now, in order to communicate Dad was given an "Etch A Sketch," a pad you can write on and then erase when you pull up the plastic cover sheet.

I went to the hospital to see Dad and to tell him I was going on a swimming outing. When I entered his hospital room, Mom and the nurses and Dad were laughing and joking; as if they were having a party. The sunny joy in that room mirrored the day outside. Dad was writing on his board and sharing what he wrote with the nurses. The nurses were buzzing around Dad like bees to honey. I never saw them so lively. When they saw me, they all swooped out like birds chirping and fluttering together.

Alone with Dad, I told him I didn't think I was doing very well in biology. It was hard for me. Then he wrote these words to me on his "Etch A Sketch." "Patti, you can do anything you put your mind to." I was lifted and encouraged into a new way of thinking. I knew that he really believed this about me, and his belief created a new belief in me. I never forgot his words. Dad was different that day. He was expansive, happy, free. It seemed like he was getting better. I kissed him goodbye and assured him I'd be back in the morning to relieve Mom.

The details of my time at the pool are muted, like looking at life from under the water. I took a swimming lesson from the guard, but I felt like I couldn't breathe, couldn't get my air, like I might drown. I remember lying on the cement on the side of the pool, resting there, trying to catch my breath, trying to find a way to relax. Seeing all the kids running and playing and laughing was surreal. Lying on my back on the cement, my cousin Connie noticed me there and appeared to me as if in a fish-eye lens. She bent over me to ask if I was okay.

On July 9, I couldn't wake up. It was like I was drugged with sleep, drowning in quicksand. I finally threw myself into getting ready to go to the hospital and relieve my Mom, but at 11:30 a.m., Mom met me in the dining room, my favorite room, the beautiful room with the lead glass windows fanning prisms of light everywhere. Mom faced me there on that spot, in that room, and said, "It's okay. You don't have to go to the hospital. Dad died this morning." That room where we met forever after reminded me of the cavern that opened up that day and swallowed me into the bowels of the earth. Ironically, it was that same room where Mom would take her final breath years later.

Mom hugged me and we cried, but inside I was in shock. I never knew he was dying! No one said he was terminal. No one had prepared me for this moment. I thought he was getting better. Yesterday he had seemed transformed. Later I learned that people can rebound right before the end and appear to be getting better. Surrendering to the inevitability of death before them can bring a transcendent freedom and relief, perhaps a sense that the pain is finally over. I believe that surrender is what released Dad that sunny day.

At first, I blamed myself. I should've been there with him. If only I could've gotten there when I said I would, then I would have been there for him. I was lost and bereft, mystified about not knowing the truth, and heartbroken at his leaving me and not being able to be with him and say goodbye. I felt my father had been stolen from me.

Back then I didn't know about cancer. I never experienced anyone else who had it. I didn't know it was almost always a death sentence in those days. Without any discussion or information I naturally assumed that Dad would recover the way anyone else did after being sick. In my experience, sick people got well again.

At that time, much of these emotions and thoughts were hidden. I didn't know how angry I was at him for leaving me and for not knowing the truth of his condition. My guilt for not being with him was also tremendous. It took years to identify and understand these feelings and to come to some resolution about them. I now know that guilt and anger are a normal part of grief and loss. Over the years I have come to trust in a divine order. My inability to wake up or get up that morning was really a blessing. I wasn't supposed to be with Dad when he died.

Over the years, I've come to know that it is the dying person's choice as to how, when, and with whom they die. It is a personal choice that is connected with their soul's ultimate process. Their choice is designed with the particular need of their own soul being of utmost importance.

I know of a dying person who had his family hovering around him in the hospital for weeks, never leaving him alone. Finally, when the family took a walk down the hall, the person died. Their absence made it easier for him to let go. Sometimes the hold of the living is just too strong for the soul to be able to leave. That man's soul needed him to die alone, and we may never know the full reason it had to happen that way.

Yet even as children we know on some level what is going on. Without a context about death and dying, I couldn't completely put it together by myself but I now see my experience at the pool as a clear inner knowing in the form of a somatic embodiment in myself of what I felt about Dad's tracheotomy. It was a shock to me. So at the pool, I experienced what it feels like to have difficulty breathing like what he must have felt. This was my unconscious desire to understand and process the extreme surgery that robbed my father of his ability to speak.

How ironic that he lost his speech because as a family, we didn't speak to each other about the reality of what was happening nor did we share our feelings about it. We just avoided the truth of what was really going on all around us. My father was only hours away from death and I couldn't breathe. Yet the unspoken family guideline still prevailed.

After Dad died the balance of our family naturally changed. I visually understood us as equal sides of a triangle—Mom, my brother Chip and me supporting and counting on each other to survive in this new configuration, this new family system.

Being five and a half years older than Chip, I sometimes felt like his little mother and took my responsibility for him very seriously. It was often my job, given to me by Mom, to make sure her orders were carried out fully when I was baby-sitting the young Chip. I believed that Mom would not abide any wiggle room, or flimsy interpretation of her words when I was placed as a child myself in charge of this precious life. So if Mom said, "Put him to bed at 9:00 p.m.," I could not allow him to be up at 9:05 p.m. on my watch.

Years later a college boyfriend visiting our home at Thanksgiving remarked that Chip seemed to be my fourteen year-old father because he was quizzing him about his prospects in life and his intentions toward me. As is often the case in families after the death of a father, the boy is unfairly made to take on the manly responsibilities of the family and home. This can create a difficult path for a young man and forces him to attempt to be mature and responsible for the family before he is ready. It can steal his youth. Both my brother and I became "parentified children" and lost some of our youth and freedom.

I loved Chip deeply. We held a shared history together from the day of his birth and we were always close, helping each other to get through life in the best way we could imagine. Our relationship has grown into a source of support and thoughtfulness and the blessing of a trusted friend. The words, "my Brother" are sacred words to me as is the sound of Chip calling me, "Sis."

## FATHER IS

My brother's eyes shine, glimpsing magical,
mysterious firelight in his baby boy,
seeing the luminescence of this little one's being
through his own soul's mirror image
    bounced back and forth
between father and son.

Slowly my brother is beginning to turn around,
to look over his shoulder
    into the face of our father
lost to us at fifty-six.

Although the first looking, at his son, was miraculous,
this second glance, at his father, is more elusive.
There is the distance of time
and the difference of dimensional planes,
    yet a silvery shimmer of connection remains.
Father is.

But where is father?
How do you find one so long absent?

I see him so clearly in dreams, in images of home.
I have words, pictures, memories stored in my heart:
    at Delaware Lake shadowed by towering oak trees
       sledding down snow-packed hills,
          giggling, clinging to his back for life;
    in his barber shop
       spinning me on his imposing barber chair,
          exotic talc wafting in circles around me;
    in his closet

touching neatly hanging silky ties
    with the unmistakable fresh scent that is Dad;
on our walks,
    trying to keep up with his long strides,
      a smile in his eyes
        as he sings in his gentle, light voice
        "Margie" and "I'm Forever Blowing Bubbles."
I see him lift his newborn, chunky-cheeked son,
    kissing him,
      celebrating him.

Father is now in the shape of my brother's eyes,
in his face and in his smile,
    in the way he moves
and in some of his thoughts.

I watch this unfolding of father to son, son to father
mirrors facing mirrors,
reflecting their images into infinity.
I am powerless in this rite of identification,
    but I long for my brother's fulfillment
and for my own.

## The Don't Talk Rule

The "Don't Talk" rule is based in the fear of upsetting children, of diverting their attention from their studies, muddying their play, obliterating their innocence and their childhood. How do you communicate with your little ten year old son and fifteen year old daughter that someone they love is dying? Our culture at the time taught that children should not be told about death. They need to be protected from this trauma by silence. "What they don't know won't hurt them," became the guiding adage.

People also choose to remain silent for fear of not knowing how to process deep sadness in children or in themselves. Was it frightening to imagine having to deal with my reactions, whatever they might be? Were my family members unsure how to be with my feelings, my pain, my disappointment, my anger, my numbness, my disbelief?

I know my parents believed they were trying to do what was best for us, and I do not blame them but this withholding of the facts of my father's dying eliminated the necessary expression and processing of feelings, and plunged my brother and me into years of confused bereavement. There was no place for my anger, feelings of betrayal, shock, disbelief or anything other than sadness. And even sadness had to be contained.

Not being told about my father's dying had major consequences. I was not able to ask questions or understand the dying process; I felt like an outsider unable to come to a resolution alongside of the rest of the family. I was kept from facing the reality of life on life's terms. Perhaps the most hurtful was not having the chance to say goodbye to my one and only beloved father. All of this placed a stamp of confusion and dissociation during a significant formative period in my life.

Family secrets are harmful when someone in the family is kept from the truth. Even children have a clear sense of inner knowing. When those you love and trust don't speak truth, they give the unspoken impression that there is nothing to worry about, nothing should be mentioned or discussed, no needs or feelings should be expressed. Yet, because you still sense the truth, logically you can only begin to doubt yourself. You start to doubt what you saw, felt, sensed. At times, you even doubt your sanity.

Family secrets undermine your security. It can feel like your internal world has turned colorless and upside-down. Family secrets clog up access to your own soul.

In the days, weeks, months after Dad's death, time was a blur to me. I had great difficulty falling asleep. In that space of aloneness, I didn't need to keep up any pretense but I'm sure the letting go into sleep brought up again and again the shocking loss of hearing my father was dead.

I found the only way to comfort myself was to pray the rosary of my Catholic upbringing. These prayers were so familiar and rote that they had a calming effect, a meditative peacefulness. I kept the rosary on my bedpost, and it was my soul's comfort in that desperate darkness.

At night while I cried, I heard my little brother Chip, crying in his bedroom to my left and I could hear Mom crying in her bedroom to my right. What a lonely scene of such unshared grief. But because of the "Don't Talk" rule that pervaded our lives, we each suffered alone in our own separate hells.

After a lifetime of learning, I know now that we must find the courage to speak our truth and include any and all feelings in what sometimes becomes a messy mix. Our self-expression is our path to freedom.

Death and dying is the greatest taboo of modern society. Submerged in a sea of our own culture, we can barely distinguish the norms and prevailing beliefs and practices that encase us and dictate the limitations of our lives. We may have difficulty at times even mentioning the word, death. Instead we try to minimize or pretty it up with all sorts of euphemisms: she's left us, he's gone over to the other side, she's met her maker, he's laid to rest, she's pushing up daisies, he bit the dust, she gave up the ghost, he was taken away, she's in the great beyond, he bought the farm, she's six feet under, he's a goner. And my personal favorite—he kicked the bucket.

Dying and even aging are seen as the enemy. We spend billions of dollars just to erase wrinkles, to look as if we will live forever. Medicine's overriding intention is to keep people alive at all costs. The death of a patient is often viewed as a failure of medicine to prolong life.

By denying and fearing death, a natural part of life is repressed and when this happens strange behaviors emerge. Violence in our society and images of death and violence seem to dominate movies, television and video games. Recently there is a series of movies about vampires. People can't seem to get enough of this bizarre and frightening way to avoid death through an unnatural life.

Death can seem like the ultimate enemy. In one respect, how could death be anything but an enemy? An enemy is something or someone against us. Whatever annihilates our loved one, or erases our own life, therefore can be seen as our enemy.

Of course, everyone will die someday. The six billion of us must eventually vacate the premises to leave room for the ones who will come after us. Death is a normal part of life, not an unanticipated mistake. We come to life to learn and teach and when we have completed what we came to do, we can graduate to a higher school of learning and contribution. Death is not our enemy.

How we face death shapes our life. A life surrounded by death makes life instantly more compelling. Each day takes on a poignancy when we realize we never really know which moment might be our last.

When facing death, it is impossible to avoid what is true. Death shows us in crystal clarity that we all have a limited amount of precious time on earth. In that awareness every moment becomes an unrepeatable gift, never to return again. How this awareness informs your life, plans and actions is based on whether or not you choose to explore the beliefs and practices that we as a culture have blindly adopted, and to break the code of denial and fear about death that it teaches.

As I accepted death, I embraced life. I fell in love with the world. The more I faced the impermanence in all things, the more dearly I valued life.

I found that in the presence of a person dying, there is such a tender preciousness. Watching a loved one breathe his or her next breath, being in the intimate presence of that person, choosing to serve this being, makes every touch of a hand a miracle of life. Every kindness shared is a symphony. Every day that the sun rises and bathes the world in light is an epiphany.

Because this could be the last time, the last breath, the last moment, life itself becomes an unspeakably magnificent event. In facing death, there is not a single breath to waste. Every breath, every prayer, every conversation can reveal a moment of grace, healing, creation. Facing death informs our life. Can we remain awake enough to remember to use our one amazing life in such a sacred way? Unless our life includes death, we will be face to face with numbing fear about our own life, and unresolved and confusing grief in the loss of others.

## OUR LOST FATHERS

So many of us have lost our fathers…
> through death—because men often die earlier than women,
> or through divorce—some become "Dead-beat Dads"
> or work—they are programmed to be the "breadwinner"
> or silence—as boys they are taught to be stoic
> or too much alcohol, drugs, gambling, overeating, or other women

or through dominance—breaking our spirit
or not strong enough—tolerating too much
or unresponsive to injustices and suffering
or through hurtful touches
or no touching at all
or too busy, too scared, or too angry
to remain in our lives.

I mourn for all of my brothers who lost their opportunity to have a positive role model of manhood.

I mourn for all my sisters who received confused messages from their absent Dad. Did your Dad show you how loved you are, how special and important you are? Have you noticed the way he treated you could set up an unconscious expectation in you as to how other men in your life should treat you in that same way?

I mourn for all our mothers who have lost their life partner, their closest friend and support system, and still do their best to balance being both mother and father, nurturer and breadwinner for their children.

I mourn for all our fathers who had no father of their own or were products of a culture which taught them to hide their emotions, be strong, do their duty, and a million other dictates that keep them from balance, from remembering to play, from their soft places, and their strengths, from the full spectrum of feelings. Don't let those "shoulds" keep you from discovering how to live life not as a "prescribed role" but as a multi-dimensional being.

Blessings on all people, who found some way to dismantle the acculturation that tried to keep them in confinement. Blessings on you who have at least begun to find your voice, your feelings, your truth, your authentic power, your unique unrepeatable beauty, your magnificence. I honor your struggle, your process, your triumph.

## Finding Closure

"You would know the secret of death?
How shall you find it unless you seek it in the heart of life?
If you would indeed behold the spirit of death,
Open your heart wide unto the body of life.
For life and death are one,
Even as the river and the sea are one."

*The Prophet*, by Kahlil Gibran

Every moment of life presents us with the choice to embrace death or not. Some moments present this choice with indelible strokes.

A few years ago, I attended a lecture by a woman who had been widowed as a result of a terrorist bomb exploding on Pan Am flight 103 over Lockerbie, Scotland on December 21, 1988. All 259 people on board the plane died, and 11 people on the ground were also killed.

The widow told us many stories. One story was about a man who was lost off of Key West in a boating accident. His body was never recovered and his wife was unable to move on with her life. Her life was on hold, always waiting for him to turn up. How could she really be sure that he was dead? She made up stories. He wasn't on that boat. Perhaps he sailed away to a distant land. Her mind kept alive the many things that could have happened and those thoughts kept her in limbo.

The speaker said when what was left of the bodies from the passengers on the Pan Am flight were found and assembled, each of the family members was given a choice whether to see the remains of their loved one or not. The bodies were in pieces. Sometimes there was just the lower leg and foot peeking out of a body bag.

I imagine fear and trepidation accompanied the families as they made their decision whether to see their loved one's remains or not. The speaker said about half of the families chose to look and half chose not to look. The families have had times of coming together over the years, and she reported that ten years after the bombing, those who chose to see their loved one's remains were resolving their grief and those who chose not to look, were still in deeply unresolved and complicated grief. These people seemed to be stuck in the past and were still struggling to believe that their loved one had really died.

If they couldn't believe that their loved one was dead, they didn't accept death, so they couldn't move forward in their grieving process from grief and denial into anger, bargaining, depression and finally acceptance. These are the five stages of grief popularized by the pioneer in death and dying studies, Dr. Elisabeth Kubler-Ross. The families were stuck in incompletion.

No one really can know what they would do if faced with the same situation. I'm sure the families who chose not to look reasoned that their choice would help them recover more easily. Most of us would want to see our loved one, hold them, kiss them, speak to them. Certainly we would want this if they were living. But now that they have died, the survivors might have no idea what to expect as they faced a corpse. I wonder if they thought they might be further traumatized by seeing a dismembered part of their precious loved one.

Can you see that how the families made their choice must have been based on their beliefs about and relationship with death? Hopefully we will be spared ever having to make such a choice. Yet what else might we find distasteful or unnatural in the dying process that is ours to witness?

During the early part of my life, I also believed that the best thing to do with all of my losses was simply to endure, to soldier through, to do the necessary action in burying the dead and move on, continuing to live to the best of my ability. I began to discover this plan was woefully lacking as each unresolved death took up more and more of my breathing room.

Is there really such power and meaning in closure? I know that there is. Without closure, both the dying person and the survivors are alone and abandoned. Looking squarely at and through death can be healing.

I encourage you to courageously take a look at death. It won't harm you and it could set you free. You are stronger than death. Don't turn away. Embrace death as a part of life that we will all experience. If you don't deal with death, unfinished business will continue to haunt you until you do.

In a grief processing group that I joined several years after my father's death, a friend of mine shared that she was angry at her father for dying and leaving her. Up to that point I wasn't consciously aware of my own anger about my father's death. Anger can often be so misunderstood. Logically I knew my father didn't want to die, didn't purposely wish to leave us. But hearing my friend express her anger gave me permission to unlock my own feelings and I began to get clearer about my father's death. I came to understand that abandonment through death is as real as any other experience of abandonment. Of course, it was not my Dad's intention to leave us, but intentional or not, he did leave.

My process began by simply acknowledging and being with my loss. My parents' choice to withhold the fact that

Dad was dying was meant to protect us; yet I felt lied to and betrayed. I was robbed of being able to say goodbye, to have closure, to cry with my Dad, to express whatever needed to be expressed, to tell him I loved him, to hear him express his love, and to deal with the reality of his death actually occurring.

I must have been confused and upset, but there was no space for me to even admit it to myself. I had to swallow it. My role was to be the bigger person. With all the preparations for the funeral, I had to support Mom and do what I thought I was supposed to do: keep it together, appear to be fine, and go on. Certainly if there was no space to express my feelings before Dad died, there was even less space after.

I don't remember ever crying again with Mom after she shared with me that Dad died. We all held in our tears until we were alone in our beds. There was one notable exception. After we said prayers at Dad's grave site, on the way to the limousine, Mom broke down. She could no longer contain her grief. I was in the presence of a woman, not just my mother, who cried for the loss of the love of her life and the sound of her deep agony and despair broke my heart. Someone caught her and steadied her and helped her into the limo. I never heard her cry like that before or since.

## Funerals and Celebration of Life Services

"To us the ashes of our ancestors are sacred, and their resting place is hallowed ground."

Chief Seattle, 1885

There is a trend lately that the bereaved may be more comforted by having a memorial service which celebrates the life of the deceased. The growing number of celebration of life services signifies an important shift in focus from funereal despair into honoring a person's earthly walk and celebrating all they did in life from the relationships they forged to their career achievements and everything in between. In these gatherings, the full expression of feelings is encouraged and it is as normal to pass the tissues as it is to laugh out loud at a humorous memory.

Both celebration of life and funeral services are important and helpful to the survivors. I have seen these ending ceremonies create an energy of closure that lifts the survivors' grief to a shared peacefulness and facilitates a release from holding onto the loved one to letting them go. This closure is crucial for being able to move on.

It seems that we need to follow nature in this. Wouldn't it seem odd to the natural world in places that have four seasons if we jumped from spring and summer back to spring again without time for the trees to turn colors and the snow to cover the world in a blanket of rest? It is just as unnatural to lose a loved one and then jump back into everyday life without time to say goodbye.

How do we say goodbye to someone already dead?

Because the closure process is so beyond the everyday, I have found that rituals are a way to contain this tumultuous loss, because they transcend the ordinary and create a united expression of emotion.

In these services there can be powerful support from the remaining family and friends. Family and friends can help each other to find comfort in being together by sharing memories, prayers, and songs that show how much their loved one meant. There's great power in speaking the stories of a person's life. Often those gathered discover some new awareness through those shared stories. As the Dutch Proverb says,

> "Shared joy is doubled joy,
> Shared grief is halved grief."

Seeing the body is important, as I've mentioned. We had an open casket at my Mother's wake and they let the family come in to view the body before the rest of the people arrived. As I entered the viewing room, I didn't know how I could gaze on my mother's face again. I had spent so much time watching her in her final days, I feared that seeing her face would ignite overwhelming sadness once again. So with trepidation, I took my sister-in-law, Barbara's hand for support as we entered the room. When I got close enough to see Mom lying in the casket, I snapped forward. My Mom's essence wasn't there. She was gone. All that remained was the body devoid of her spirit. It was so obvious that the essence of what made her who she was in life was completely free and released.

## The Give-Away

Sometimes other cultures can show us a ritual or a practice that can help us to heal the loss that may seem beyond words.

In the culture of many Native Americans, after the loss of a loved one, a family will offer possessions to the rest of the community as part of the grieving process. The "give-away" is done with joy as a means of healing. It is a sharing from the heart. The gifts are given freely and, in this way, the life and death of their loved one makes a direct difference to the rest of the community. This generosity demonstrates that the loved one mattered and existed for a larger reason; even in death they are a support to others in the community. Recipients of the gift know that it doesn't carry any strings with it. It is given with no expectations. The new owners can do with the gifts whatever they choose. The giver knows that all that is given will come back to them in various ways, in other forms of good.

A friend of mine created a similar ritual when her sister died. Her sister was quite young and beloved by the community and many people mourned her loss. The surviving sister invited friends to an afternoon open house where people casually stopped in and shared food. All were invited to take whatever they wanted of the sister's jewelry, clothes and books. It was a lovely time of remembering and reminiscing together in community the love of this woman as we gently touched and shared her possessions. Now her friends often wear the woman's clothes and jewelry and her sister says it gives her such joy to see reminders of her beloved sister displayed. It's as if she sees her sister all around her and it has become a meaningful way for the community to remember her.

## Forgiveness

Sometimes it helps in our grieving process to speak directly and forgive our loved ones, even if they have left this earth. The format of a letter is one way to compose our thoughts.

*Dear Dad and Mom,*

*What a devastating time this must have been for both of you. It would have been quite enough to cope with Dad's dying, but at the same time there was also the illness and death of Dad's eldest brother, Anthony, and the diagnosis of Parkinson's disease and the experimental, excruciating medical procedure performed on Dad's closest brother, Sam.*

*I so wish we all could have been there for each other. Perhaps sharing with me, Dad, might have been helpful to you, too. I'm sad that neither of us was able to say goodbye. I know what you wrote to me on the "Etch A Sketch" was meant to be something I could carry with me and remind me who you were to me. I am deeply grateful to have your*

25

*words of encouragement, and that statement has made a difference in my life. When I think of what you wrote, I am in touch with your love.*

*It is not always easy, but I have found how important it is to be a truth seeker and a truth speaker.*

*I do absolutely forgive you both for being unable to share your grief with me and being unaware of my need for that sharing.*

*Love,*
*Patricia*

# SACRED PROCESS

## YOUR OWN ACCULTURATION

1. Describe your first experience of death. Include animals as well as human beings. What emotions and beliefs did you have as a result?
2. What did your parents, teachers, religion tell you about death and dying?
   Was death a comfortable topic for discussion in your home?
3. How easy is it for you to talk about death and dying now? Compare your response with your parents' ability to discuss death with you or each other.
4. Have you ever seen a dead body? What did you observe about it? Did it frighten you? If you had to identify a loved one's body after a traumatic death, would you agree to look at it?
5. Should death be faced, or ignored and avoided?
6. Is death so scary you shouldn't look at it, or is it a natural part of life?
7. Is closure important? Is saying goodbye in a complete and meaningful way a crucial part of being able to begin again?
8. Is it important and necessary to witness our loved one's dead body and observe that the vital part of them, the soul, the part that animated flesh, is gone, no longer within their body? Is it important to honor the body, to bless it and release it, and thank it for carrying the precious soul all the years of its life?

# CHAPTER 2

# Befriending Your Feelings

"Get ready to weep tears of sorrow as bright as
the brightest beads, and like the bright beads
you string to wear round your throat at the
burial, gather your tears and string them on
a thread of your memory to wear around your
heart or its shattered fragments will never come
whole again."

— *LONELINESS*, BY CLARK E. MOUSTAKAS

"Give sorrow words; the grief that does not
speak whispers the o'er-fraught heart and bids
it break."

— *MACBETH*, BY WILLIAM SHAKESPEARE

## Three Uncles

MY THREE UNCLES, Mike, Sam and Joe all died difficult deaths
in the 1970s and early 1980s. Witnessing their experiences
taught me about choices we all face in illness and end of life
care and brought up many painful emotions.

## Unfinished Business: Uncle Joe

Uncle Joe, my Dad's older brother, was one of my favorite uncles. When I was a little girl, Uncle Joe wanted me to have a puppy. Apparently he believed a pet was very important in a child's life. He even went so far as to give my parents money to purchase a cocker spaniel, the type of dog that he discovered would be most compatible with a child. Unfortunately, we lived in an apartment that didn't allow pets. So I never received a sweet puppy of my own, but I always remembered that loving and thoughtful gesture from my Uncle Joe.

Uncle Joe was a robust and warm man who was our occasional babysitter in our early years. Whenever Uncle Joe would come to baby-sit, he'd bring lobster tails and we would all feast together on this delicacy that Mom would prepare before she and Dad went out for their time alone.

After Uncle Joe put us to bed, my little brother and I couldn't contain ourselves. We would sneak out of bed and creep up to right behind Uncle Joe's chair in the TV room. We faced the mixed joy and terror of having him discover us and jump to his feet to order us back to bed with the full force of his sergeant's command. I think he secretly enjoyed playing our game too.

Uncle Joe had been a career sergeant in the Marines and participated in some of the bloodiest battles in the Pacific Campaign during the storming of Iwo Jima Island against Japan during World War II. The battle of Iwo Jima was the first attack on the Japanese homeland and the longest and most intense conflict in the Pacific theatre. The reports say that the coarse volcanic sand beach where the American Marines landed flowed with so much blood for the thirty-six day battle, that it turned the black sand red.

I never heard stories about Uncle Joe's experiences in his military career, but I had a sense of the unresolved horror he must've carried all his life when Mom and I went to visit him during the last days of his life at the Veteran Affairs (VA) hospital. Uncle Joe was dying of cancer. When we arrived at his bedside, he was having flashbacks of the war. I was shocked to witness my Uncle Joe screaming battle cries, as if he were in a firefight.

"Look out!" He was yelling commands to his soldiers, completely oblivious of my mother's and my presence. The battle was real and immediate to him and yet he lay in front of us in a hospital bed.

I was deeply saddened to realize that those traumas were not healed and were still alive in him after all those years. He carried those memories all his adult life, for decades, reliving the horror of war, tortured in dreams and flashbacks with no respite. There was no safe place afforded to him to escape this endless misery until the only way out, his death.

The term PTSD (post-traumatic stress disorder) emerged in 1980 and since Uncle Joe died in 1971, he couldn't have received the counseling/intervention that is more available in recent times. Ed Tick, in his insightful book, *War and the Soul*, speaks with experience and wisdom of new ways beyond medication and alleged quick fixes to heal soldiers traumatized by war. Tick advocates a comprehensive treatment program that uses both EMDR (Eye Movement Desensitization and Reprocessing), a recognized form of trauma treatment which assists in unlocking the repetitive brain patterning causing flashbacks, and therapy for the parts of the personality that atrophied while being stuck in the past. This repair work includes ritual and returning to the location of where the war took place in order to rectify the present with the past. But Uncle Joe had no such assistance. I wish that my dear Uncle and others like him, could have known life free of the terror that hung unremittingly in their memories.

What a heavy burden our soldiers carry alone without treatment to help them heal their traumas of war and horrific images of death.

Yet I know that our soul is always trying to heal and bring resolution right up to the last moment even during the process of dying. I imagine that in Uncle Joe's state of "hallucinations" expressing themselves in that clouded time before death, that he might have felt unrestrained freedom to have his flashbacks and speak out loud what he couldn't speak before. My hope is that there was some touch of grace that comforted him and released him from the fear, pain and remorse for all that he experienced.

For everyone who is living with psychic wounds, from war to childhood abuse or neglect, the unfinished business can rear its ugly head as our body weakens toward death. There is help available for anyone who wants it these days. Trauma can be healed. Better to do your psychological work earlier rather than later. Find a way to tell the truth and free your heart from bondage to the past by seeking a qualified therapist.

## Uncle Mike

Uncle Mike lived with us most of my life. I'm sure my Mother felt protective of him; for it was she who, as a young woman, tracked down her brother who had been abandoned as a child by their parents and left in an orphanage in White Plains, N.Y. After finding him, Mom brought her older brother to live with our family in Buffalo. Mike had had gangrene in one leg as a child and the medical minds of that time did what they thought was the only option—amputate. However, as short sighted as that surgery was, they also miscalculated, or perhaps never considered that this little child would obviously grow. When he did grow, the stump that they left was too short to attach a prosthesis properly; so all his life, the top of the artificial leg cut into and irritated his thigh making it even harder than it would have been to walk, turn, and maneuver.

Uncle Mike never seemed to take himself too seriously though. He recounted to our family a time when he played baseball in the orphanage and decided to take off his artificial leg and use it to hit the ball and then hopped to first base.

Uncle Mike was another one of my favorite uncles. He was kind and soft spoken and generous to all the kids on the block. He'd give us money to buy ourselves treats at the corner store. Actually, if Mom didn't watch him, he'd give away all his money to almost anyone.

His pattern was to drive himself mercilessly at his job as a cook. He always did more than his share and worked overtime, all for poor wages. Someone at that time cruelly said, "It's not a problem to hire the handicapped (now more sensitively called "people with disabilities") because they usually over-compensate for their perceived lack and the boss gets more than what they would from a person without a disability." That certainly seemed to be my Uncle Mike's way.

Uncle Mike would drag himself home after each grueling day of work completely exhausted. He usually would not have eaten even though he was making food for others all day. Sometimes he'd just grab some cold spaghetti from our fridge and hibernate in his room. Work and cigarettes filled his days, and TV and a steady supply of beer comforted his nights. So it was not a surprise when he was diagnosed with cancer of the lungs and throat given his long-term pattern of ingesting toxic substances, mixed with his lack of self-care and self-love.

After lung surgery, they told Uncle Mike there was nothing more they could do to save his life. Yet, even though he was not fully recovered from that surgery, the doctors suggested doing another invasive surgery on his neck and jaw, as the cancer was discovered there too. Their master plan was to remove the right side of his jaw and part of his neck and then cut off a large piece of his skin from his hip all the way up his side. They proposed to graft this "flap," as they called it, from his shoulder to his face and wrap it around his neck to try to keep the skin alive, in hopes the "flap" would adhere. It was alarming to imagine his doctors excising more parts of his body the way other doctors took his leg early in his life, especially since they felt there was no chance of saving his life.

I wrote Uncle Mike to remind him that he could say "No" to this extreme and really futile measure. Just because they were doctors, didn't mean you had to do everything they suggest. But Uncle Mike agreed to this procedure, I believe, for two reasons. It was difficult for him to say "No" to requests, and certainly to authority figures, and perhaps the opportunity to take some action no matter how terrible toward the hope of longer life, was preferable to surrendering to death. He, like most Western people, would do whatever the "experts" recommended to stay alive. It is so foreign to many of us to say, "Enough." I tried to help my Uncle stand up to the doctor and refuse the surgery. He had every right to refuse, but he ignored my appeal. And yet, it was his choice, no one else could make it for him.

And so, the doctors performed their medical experiment. The result was horrible. The skin graft didn't adhere. "The flap" oozed puss and blood and Mike died after more mutilation and unnecessary suffering. My uncle became a living cadaver, carved up without concern for his wellbeing, his feelings, his pain and suffering, his quality of life or his impending death. This was a difficult way to die and his situation shows a lack of clarity about what was of most value to Uncle Mike. Did he really want to exhaust every medical procedure if it was not life-saving? Did he understand that he could choose to refuse more surgery so that his quality of life could take precedence in his final days? This is an important example of why it is critical to have an advanced directive and living will in place before you might need it. Uncle Mike might not have been thinking clearly and so was unable to communicate his wishes at such a difficult time.

I have heard it said that children are the only ones who can be considered to be true victims and that adults can be participants in being abused. Certainly, as adults we must take responsibility for our part in allowing abuse to happen in our lives. Yet, when I think of the childhood neglect, abandonment, and initial medical abuse that filled Uncle Mike's childhood days, I believe he was programmed to live a life of limitation, over-compensation, and passivity. Mike lived life in "learned helplessness" which is a common adaptation to abuse. By being beaten down by life, many children learn that they are powerless to take action by making positive change or standing up for themselves.

This concept of "learned helplessness" reminds me of an experiment with fleas. Fleas can easily jump several feet but when they are placed in a jar with a glass lid on it, the fleas learn that they can't jump as high as they used to anymore. They can't jump out of the jar. And even when the "ceiling" is removed, the fleas still jump only as high as that previous limit. They have "learned helplessness."

## Medical Abuse

When I was growing up, I believed like most, that doctors were gods.

Because of a huge imbalance of power, there can be conflicts of interest resulting in medical abuse. Perhaps the recommended treatment is part of their experimental research or will contribute to their personal knowledge and financial gain.

I have since discovered that this type of unnecessary surgery is occurring more often on Medicare and Medicaid patients when they are most vulnerable or near the end of their life.

Of course I know that all doctors are not like this. Most are compassionate and truly well-meaning. When an operation is called for, Western medicine can be powerful and healing. This is confirmed time and again. Yet each one of us must be awake to take responsibility for what we allow to happen to us in the name of a "cure" and to center in our own guidance without blindly following the advice of "experts."

Here's a litmus test question: if the patient deeply knows he/she has the permission and support to refuse a doctor's suggested treatment, would the patient still choose this direction? I know my uncle didn't have his own sense of internal permission and I didn't see this permission clearly encouraged by his doctor. This is why second and even third opinions are helpful and every patient has a right to ask for and receive them. Do your own research. You can ask a nurse her opinion. Today there are also many excellent resources available on-line regarding illnesses and options for treatments.

Since my Uncle Mike died in 1979, he had no access to a great movement in recent years in Western medicine for compassionate end of life care and palliative care. The goal is to improve the quality of life for the patient and the family and focuses on providing patients with relief from the symptoms and stress of a serious illness. My hope is that because palliative care is available these days, there is a better chance of experiences like Uncle Mike's being eliminated. However, we must all be alert and responsible for our care and for the care of our loved ones.

There are several layers of hospital staff whose job it is to assist and work together as a team to provide comprehensive care for the patient. For short term issues, patient advocates can help and connect patients with other resources. There are certified chaplains, and licensed social workers, and therapists who can give emotional, financial and other support. Case managers are assigned to assist in setting up further health care in another facility or at home after the patient is discharged from the hospital. Ask for the information you need and you'll feel more empowered in any decision.

Neuroscientist, Dr. Daniel Levitin, in his book, *The Organized Mind,* suggests that you ask your doctor two very important questions when faced with having to make a difficult decision regarding a proposed treatment or surgery. Levitin says that doctors and pharmaceutical companies know the answers to these questions, but may not be thrilled to share that information with the patient.

The first question that Levitin suggests is "what is the number to treat," which means what is the statistical percentage of how many people are helped by this medication or treatment? One would think that everyone would be helped in the same way, but sadly this is not the case. For example, Levitin says the statin drugs that are used to lower cholesterol have a number to treat at 300. This means that one in 300 are helped by these drugs.

The second question to ask is "what are the side effects?" With statins, five percent of the people experience major side effects of gastro-intestinal distress and debilitating muscular pain. Five percent of 300 is fifteen, so fifteen out of 300 people taking statin drugs are more likely to be harmed than helped. Of course, whether to accept any treatment is an individual decision, but with clear statistical information like this, it's easier to talk about the risks and the quality of life in order to make an informed decision.

Don't be afraid to ask questions. Bernie Siegel, author of *Love, Medicine and Miracles,* found that the people who healed from cancer were often the ones who weren't compliant, who couldn't be called the "easy patient." The ones who survived cancer demanded answers to their questions and were actively involved in their treatment. You have a right to know the answers to all your questions.

I am sad about what happened to Uncle Mike. I regret that I was powerless to change or stop the abuse of my uncle. From his miserable childhood to his torturous dying it all seemed so shockingly unnecessary. All of these complexities of feelings are normal. My work, and our work, is to resolve those feelings.

So how can we make sense of my Uncle's tragedy? What does his life and his dying say to us who remain?

1. His sacrifice will forever remind us not to let something like this happen to us. We all need to be alert and responsible about what we choose to allow in our medical care. Have an advance directive and living will on file with your doctors and give copies to your family so that they know your wishes and can advocate for you if the time comes when you can't speak for yourself.

2. We can't spend our life angrily challenging every red light in our path, but when we see injustice and abuse, we owe it to ourselves and to those we love to try and stop it.

3. An unhealed childhood has long tentacles of unrelenting influence and can cause old patterns to play out in adulthood. Yet, abuse can be healed.

**CALL AND RESPONSE**

What can I do?
Acquiesce or rage against injustice?

Both ways have felt powerless.
Is there a middle-way that allows me dignity, respect, peace?

In the space of your heart is a clear underground spring
that is wise, ever fresh and renewing,
bringing forth crystalline water
that seeps into the ground of your cells
into the ground of your being.
This depth of freshness is who you truly are.
Eternal soul, if only you had known compassion in this world,
you would have found strength in yourself.

> May all beings be centered in who they are.
> May all beings be free from suffering.
> May all beings be at peace.
> May all beings be free.

## Uncle Sam

I probably spent more time with my Uncle Sam than any of my uncles. He and my dad were the closest in their family and my immediate family spent most weekends with Uncle Sam and Aunt Mary and my four cousins. I have wonderful memories of our times together. Our play and fun was always multiplied by the number of cousins together at one time.

My Uncle Sam was a master brick layer. His occupation was hard work especially for someone with his medium stature. I wondered if he chose this trade because he was lean, tough, athletic, and strong, or did he become all that because the work and his life demanded so much of him? He was bright and entrepreneurial and angry like a coiled spring ready to pounce. It seemed to me that he willed himself through life. He encouraged his children to be athletic and they would perform exercises, headstands and acrobatics in our midst. I recall the shock of hearing about Sam having fallen off a high scaffold at work flat onto his back. When he was diagnosed with Parkinson's disease in his early 50s, my aunt and uncle and parents wondered if that trauma might have caused his illness.

Shortly after he was diagnosed with Parkinson's disease my uncle began exhibiting uncontrollable asymmetrical tremors. Uncle Sam read an article in *Life Magazine* about a renowned brain surgeon who was getting favorable results eliminating Parkinson's tremors through a new and somewhat controversial surgical procedure in NYC. The operation was considered controversial because they chose not to perform the first trials on animals as was the usual protocol, but tested these surgeries from the beginning on human beings. Uncle Sam decided to have two surgeries since the first surgery stopped the tremors on his right side. He got good results from the second surgery as the left side tremors also stopped.

To prepare for the surgery to stop his tremors, the doctors drilled four holes in his skull, using only a local anesthetic, in order to attach a vice that would hold his head completely motionless. Then a laser was used to touch certain parts of his brain where they suspected the tremors originated. In order to do so, Uncle Sam had to remain fully awake so they could observe his outstretched arm, noting any changes in the tremors. For the rest of his life, his skull never lost the indentations of those four holes.

Despite the fact that the tremors stopped, for nearly twenty years until his death in 1983, Uncle Sam lived with the progressive and other debilitating symptoms of Parkinson's disease including rigidity in the body, diminished muscular control, poor balance resulting in numerous falls, and eventual cognitive impairment mimicking Alzheimer's, another neurodegenerative disorder. His other symptoms included depression, fatigue, slurred speech that made him difficult to understand, and an inability to write.

When I think of my Uncle Sam's life and illness, I am filled with a deep, bruising sadness. He came through a troubled life of extreme loss and deprivation and yet remained a fighter. But finally in that second surgery, he gave way. My cousin told me that in her mind this was when her father died, when his spirit was no longer present. Why did my uncle give up? Perhaps the surgeries were just too much trauma, pushing his brain and body to the limit. Perhaps it was my uncle's own inconsolable loss of learning that my father, his younger brother and dearest friend, died on the same day as his surgery on July 9, 1966. As a shell of his former self, the remaining nearly twenty years were an exercise in total dependency and waiting for death to claim him. I cry for my Uncle Sam and for the suffering his illness caused in him and in my aunt and cousins.

I prefer to remember Uncle Sam from the stories I heard about him when he was a little boy and long before he experienced so much pain in his life. I imagine what he was like on the ship with his family crossing the Atlantic from Sicily to America when he was just five years old and my father was a baby under two. I can hear this wiry lad's laughter as he explores all over the ship, ebullient and untouched by the motion sickness affecting everyone else. Little Sammy is on the greatest adventure—going to the new world—with the promise of an extraordinary life ahead.

May he continue on his soul's ongoing journey even now—
> Free of pain
> Free of regrets
> Free of the past
> Free—free—free.

## Dealing with Feelings of Loss

Our emotions can be so raw in these times of another's dying and death. Illness and death call up all our frailties. Facing up to our own mortality and the possible permanent loss of a loved one can be so confusing and heart-breaking that we might prefer to find a cave to wait out the storm. But we can't.

What if we could discover instead that our emotions are our friends; that they are the language of the heart? Think of your feelings as your heart's internal wisdom speaking to you. Emotions help us by giving voice to what we need and giving us strength and resolve to take appropriate action, to do what needs to be done, throughout this morass of illness, decision-making and loss.

Many of us question the way we feel at this time, so knowing the range of possible emotions in such difficult circumstances can be reassuring and help us to identify what might be happening in our emotional space. First of all, there are many varieties of feelings and reactions to illness and death as there are people. There is no one "right" way to grieve. Each person is an individualized, unrepeatable being, so there is no linear process, and no time limit on grieving. An individual's response depends on many variables. Some, among others, are:

How close were you to your loved one?
Was their death expected or was it a sudden loss?
Did you have time to prepare yourself?
Were you able to say goodbye?

In honoring our diversity, it is important to know that not everyone feels their emotions to the same degree of intensity. The levels of intensity are very individual. Some people will welcome being able to speak about their feelings and others may resent people asking them to express feelings they don't have. Some may surprise us with how quickly they have or seem to have recovered from their loss. Both responses have strengths and limitations. Those who cry easily have strength in expressing their feelings and knowing they need support. There is also strength in being able to continue stoically through the loss and to reduce the personal pain by focusing on certain forwarding thoughts and staying active.

We grieve because we have loved. Our grief can be an indication of the depth of connection we had with our loved one. A man with little or no connection to his father barely grieved at all. He said it was hard to miss what was never there to begin with. For another, her loss included giving up the hope of ever having a meaningful relationship with her father, and this realization cause her to grieve more deeply. Another friend experienced the loss of her beloved as if she was missing an arm. Couples who live as one, who are soul mates, who feel a connection with each other perhaps even beyond this present time, may experience grief that leaves them wondering, "Who am I now?" Their very identity was entwined with their beloved. Now they have lost not only a deeply cherished person who may have filled many roles in their lives, but also have lost the one who was a major part of their identity.

When your parent dies, no matter how old you are, this loss can bring on a more complex response than other losses because, no matter what your relationship is, whether closely connected or distant, your parents are your anchor in this world. They have always been with you. So in their death, you face not only the loss of someone you care about, but you may also feel you are losing your way of being in the world. The context and background of your life has shifted. Loss can feel like an earthquake. The ground is something we expect to be supporting us, yet when the ground separates, it can be shocking and disorienting, like a parent's death.

For a while you may feel adrift because you require a new way of being in the world. What will be your new anchor? This can be a very difficult as well as a forwarding time for your own personal and spiritual growth. Some may try to find a new anchor by transferring dependence to another person. The greater opportunity is to find resources within yourself, to find your anchor within you. You may need to be alone for a while to do this reconnecting with your inner resources, with your eternal nature. As a result, all your relationships will be richer because you are more of who you have come here to be. You will find you have everything you need right within you.

When any beloved dies, other losses that have not healed may also rise to the surface. It is as if all of your losses are pinned on a clothesline. As you pin the most recent one, you can't help but jostle all the others waving in the breeze, waiting to be seen, to be attended to, to be healed and let down off that line. That is why our grief can feel bigger than the present loss. It sometimes is! Grief says, "Ok, now that I have your attention, now that your heart is broken open, let's address the unfinished business of healing your whole heart." In the same way, feeling anger can alert us to notice a pattern and remind us of other times we experienced the same thing in a relationship.

Not all emotions provide us with this opportunity for self-reflection and growth. For example, when you are joyous, do you think of all the other times in your life when you felt joy? Probably not. It seems to be the job of the "difficult" emotions to remind us of other similar events so we can become aware of patterns in our life and begin to transcend those patterns and heal. Grief needs time to unfold, and in giving yourself that attention, you honor yourself and move to a deeper understanding of your dear ones, yourself, and all of life.

How long does grieving last? Once again your individual timetable lies within you. Give yourself whatever time you need to allow the tears and any other feelings to surface. Take time off from work and other responsibilities if you need to.

Trying to resume your "normal" routine won't make the hurt disappear. Only the grieving that goes deeply into your feelings will eventually heal your heart.

In loss, it is usual to have intense sorrow, especially at the beginning. It is also normal to be stunned, distracted, forgetful, numb, agitated. You may also have physical pains in the chest, difficulty breathing, sleeping or waking up. You may not want to be with other people, or be afraid to be alone, avoid the places that bring back memories or dwell on the very places or things that make you remember. All these and other painful reactions can be so intense that they make you question if you are actually losing your mind. You may wonder how you will get through all this or if you yourself will die from grief. None of this is abnormal. Bereavement in all its variations must be respected.

Your emotional process has its own logic and cannot be predicted nor understood rationally. You may find yourself questioning why you are angry at a loved one for being sick or abandoning you, why you feel guilty for something that you had no control over, for crying for a longer time than you "should" be, for feeling numb or uncharacteristically disoriented and forgetful. None of these feelings can be explained. They simply ask us to open our hearts and welcome them in, to notice and make friends with those parts of ourselves that are uncomfortable, irrational and messy.

In all losses, grieving has its own natural unfoldment, and the rhythm of grieving can be surprising and confusing at times. One day, you may wish to stay in bed crying for a long time. The next day, you could feel refreshed, energized and even happy. How do you make sense of these dramatic emotional swings? On one hand, it doesn't feel appropriate to laugh and be happy. After all, your loved one is dead. Can these positive feelings be seen as an honoring of your grief and your loved one? Yes. All of the varieties of feelings are appropriate and good. All honest expressions help to shift the psyche into balance, into wholeness. Continue to surround yourself with life, to cultivate life, to express whatever emerges in you. No emotion will erase the love that you shared. Love is eternal.

Our emotions visit us for many reasons: to energize our actions; to release emotional pain; to clarify our personal truth; and to expand our hearts into an oneness and compassion for other beings on this human walk of life. So welcome them all—these emotions, these friends, these extensions of our souls. Let them come to feel at home in your expanding heart. Identify them; call them by name. Welcome terror. Welcome grief. Welcome numbness. Welcome anger. Welcome tears. Welcome guilt. Welcome them all. Through noticing, processing, discovering your own needs and taking action, you can finally come to accept and release what is happening to you. As uncomfortable as all these expressions can be, I invite you to get on good terms with them. They are part of you and can bring great blessings.

## As Time Passes

Although no one grieves in exactly the same way or within the same time frame, I have noticed some generalizations that may give you a sense of what is possible. There may be an initial period of deep sorrow and a buffer period of numbness or denial right after the loss. This buffer period seems to be designed to help us get through the initial shock so we can deal with life a bit more easily than if we were deeply in sadness during this time.

Around six months after a loss, I have at times observed a renewed grief and sadness emerge. Perhaps the psyche has had a bit of time to strengthen during this period and is ready to face reality more completely. A fear of one's own mortality may emerge at this time as well.

Then at two years, a window of further personal transformation can occur, sometimes by developing an illness. This could be seen as an indication of unfinished psychological work. Perhaps there is more to resolve in your relationship with the deceased; perhaps there is a need to reclaim your power; perhaps forgiveness is required; perhaps there is a need to delve deeper into spirituality.

Especially at this time, the survivor can come to a new awareness of their own spiritual life. There is energy in this time for great strides in personal development. Your heart has been broken open and you hunger to know about the Spirit that is within your loved one and within you and in all of us. Your own spirituality may have helped you to face your loss and can be reassuring, but sometimes the old forms may not have been enough and you find yourself demanding more answers to the big questions of what this life really means and why we are here. The culmination of all your emotional processing and reclaiming personal work can create a very fertile and productive time, adding deeper understanding and appreciation of the meaning of life.

Normal grief seems to include facing your loss as well as working to get back to developing a new life and a new identity without your loved one. I think of grief like the rain. Some days are a drizzle and then there are days that are perfectly dry. Some days bring a good cleansing deluge that shakes the drain spouts. Remember there will also be days of mellow sun with echoes of humor, memories of good times and laughter. It's all part of grieving. People can walk past this time into the future with new or renewed confidence and strengths and resources that they never dreamed were possible.

Patricia Gulino Lansky

# Expressions of Loss

## 1. FEAR

Sometimes fear washes over you.
Blasts of steam
sweep your body from toe to head.
Tiny skin hairs on alert.
Shoulders round
to shield you from attack.

Sometimes fear sneaks up on you.
Walking at night through windy woods
all the leaves are gone
yet out of the indigo air
one noiselessly lands
on the nape of your neck.

The mind can descend
onto endless precarious ledges.
The farther we stray
the worse it gets.
What if, what if, what if…
Catastrophe lies ahead.

Each path produces panic.
It could all crash!
At the edge of these possibilities
the abyss is the inevitable next step
encasing the mind in sticky webs
that restrict and suffocate.

Stop the next dire thought.
Replace it with trust in the essential goodness
found within all things.
A secret passageway can now open.
    You are lighter.
    All is in order.

## 2. SHOCK

*Did someone open my door?*
Catapulted awake,
unfocused eyes search
illuminated clock—3 a.m.

Body immobilized, mind racing
breath muffled, skin watchful
ears straining.
*An intruder in my inner domain?*

*It can't be so.*
Weighted body pulls me back toward sleep,
back to that pillowed cranny I've carved out,
so familiar, so serene.

But no, I am awake,
my comfort interrupted and all my plans.
Pounding cries echo through my brain—
*No! It can't be true!*

Vision spirals, closes like a camera lens,
ceiling slinks lower, no air,
my body caught between red alert
and the numbing dread of truth.

They said she is dying.
But I won't let her die,
not now, not yet,
not when there is so much for her to do.

## Accepting Death, Embracing Life

Not when there is so much for her to witness,
to give me the help I need,
guidance, companionship, conversations,
her laughter and wisdom, her history, home.

Surely I die too
that part of me so entwined with the
being that birthed me into being,
yet I remain alive.

I must pull myself from my pillow's folds, do what I can
my insides slung over my shoulder,
carrying my roots
like an air plant.

### 3. SADNESS

Some people are afraid of sadness.
They only want to talk about happy times.
People afraid of sadness
often apologize for their tears.
I feel sad when, muffling their truth in tissues, they say,
*I'm sorry, sorry I'm crying.*

Shared tears creates a sacred connection,
a closeness of trust, of honesty, of oneness.
Have you ever been cradled in another's arms,
held in your shared grief?
Together it doesn't seem as sad or desperate
as being there alone.

My Mother held me after she told me of her death sentence.
We cried together.
I will always remember the feeling during those moments
of how much we loved each other.
She opened her heart to share her sadness
carving a place of tenderness in both of us.

## 4. RAGE

Didn't we cheer when Dylan Thomas
demanded of his father,
*Do not go gentle into that good night?*
Then why are we surprised, hurt or rejected
when our loved one
splatters us with screams,
spits out the pill,
dismisses a guiding hand
answers our soft query
snarling, *I can do it myself.*

Are they not raging, raging
against the dying of the light?

With gnawing emptiness
missed opportunities, dangling ends
unremitting pain, diminished senses
overwhelming weakness, unspoken sadness
not wanting to be too much
yet needing what seems immense
terror of the unknown, ill-prepared
for the greatest adventure
or greatest disappointment ahead—
Rage, why not rage?

If you believe death ends our glory and our disgrace,
will your time end in rage?

## 5. GRIEF

I wade through swirling white foam
laughing, jumping in dark, dense surf.
Catching a wave, instantly I am upside down
not knowing which way is the surface,
which way holds my oxygen.
Indifferent, the wave rolls on,
tossing me like an egg beater.
All alone, heart racing, fighting,
eyes wide seeing only black,
with no sense of movement at all.

Suddenly I'm dropped on the shore,
weighted down, graceless,
shaking with fear, lungs sucking air,
hot salt tears swallowed in sand,
safe, yet angry and embarrassed,
grateful, yet horrified.
It's not fair!
I have spent enough time in grief.
I want to get on with my life
without the dread of repeat performances.
When will it be
finished?

# Accepting Death, Embracing Life

Everyone else is frolicking by the sea.
Once more, I am upside down in a black wave,
thrown down in wet sand
like a clump of tangled seaweed.
Will I ever again glide happy and carefree
skim the surface with long, easy strokes?
Will I once more languish on my back seeing sky,
legs fluttering while slow, graceful arms
dip into the water,
arching up and back.

## 6. HOPE

Sometimes the hardest thing is not knowing
like just at the start of spring
we see the first tiny buds popping up
but then the cold, wintry days return.

Why would nature play with us
if not to shake loose our hold on the knowing
like those delicate blossoms
scattered on the ground by the icy wind and rain?

Our grip on the knowing
loosens
as we are shaken after times of feeling strong
followed by times of retching and pain.

But there are times of glory in all that
moments of forgiveness
moments of belly-aching, glass-shattering laughter
moments of exquisite tenderness and honesty
that unfurl hearts.

There are also sarcastic, nasty, frustrated moments of rage
when there is nothing but hopeless power-less-ness
when no one can change the course.
Who wants to be fully in that moment?

And yet, in the center of it all
is a secret door, beyond the end-time.

# Accepting Death, Embracing Life

Do I have the courage to go there
to forgive again
to understand another's pain, to open my heart
to love another time?

Then, in an instant
the returning sun
dries the April rain
and the warmed world is spring again.

## Guilt and Regret

People sometimes make the mistake of saying, "I feel guilty," or "I feel regret." Guilt and regret are technically not emotions. They are limiting thoughts, and dwelling in those thoughts can sap our life energy because it's impossible to change what did or didn't happen in the past. If we feel guilty for some past behavior, it's important to neither excuse nor exaggerate the gravity of the error. We all make mistakes. We aren't perfect. If we harmed another, we can make amends. The Twelve-Step programs are the basis of excellent addiction recovery practices. They include an eighth step that encourages participants to "make a list of all persons we have harmed and become willing to make amends to them all." And the ninth step states, "Made direct amends to such people wherever possible, except when to do so would injure them or others."

Guilt and regrets are burdens that keep us from living life fully in the present. Our thoughts are filled with "should've, would've, could've." If only I insisted that he see the doctor sooner. If only I said those things that I wanted to say. If only I got there to be with her before she could no longer understand me. The list goes on, but the feelings underneath the thoughts include powerlessness, sorrow, and even anger. Sometimes the caregiver feels helpless, impotent, not wanted, not needed, not able to do much for the loved one, but deeply wants to make them happy. It can be difficult to accept the reality of what "is" and what we have no control over.

My friend had difficulty watching his wife continue to over-eat and repeatedly choose the wrong foods for her heart condition. He tried to change her, help her, but eventually learned to accept that his wife's body and her health were her responsibility. Even though the thought of losing her and living without her was terrifying to him, he realized he was powerless to change her, and he learned to "let go and let God." He let go of trying to control the outcome and left her daily choices and practices in his wife's hands, and in God's. Guilt and regrets occur when we want to control or prevent something from happening that is impossible to control, when we neglect to do something, or we miss an important opportunity to say or do something we wish we had done.

Sometimes we may lose a loved one suddenly, without warning. Sometimes we have the mixed blessing of time during a longer dying process. Either way, it is up to us to stay in the present with all our relationships. It is absolutely possible to have no regrets when death comes. It takes a commitment to keeping current with what we need to say, to cleaning up our messes and making amends quickly. When a loved one is ill, you can do and say everything you want to in order to tie up loose ends as long as your disclosure doesn't bring unnecessary added pain to a dying person.

I found a type of workbook that was called *A Keepsake Journal*. (There are many journals of this nature available today.) The book had questions designed to spur conversations about a person's life. I found questions like, "Tell about a favorite memory from your childhood," or "What do you feel was your greatest accomplishment?" It is a blessing to a dying person to have someone witness their life, to know that someone heard and knew who they were and that somehow their story will go on.

Have those talks, and begin them early and often. Clear up misperceptions, heal whatever needs to be healed, forgive and release and complete any unfinished business together. Tell the person you love them, if that is your truth. Leave nothing undone. Act as if this is the last day. Be in the present—the present is really the only time we have. The past is over and the future hasn't come yet. Love is the only thing that is important. Create times of sharing and unconditional love. Listen without judgment or criticism. Mostly SIT and LISTEN. Let the ears of your heart lead you in everything you do with and for your loved one.

# Holding Paradox
"I came that they may have life, and have it abundantly."
John 10:10

I came to realize in the midst of my deepest sadness, a sadness that I felt through my entire body and mind, that the Truth of the soul is also present in me. For my loved one, as well as myself, the larger umbrella over all the grief is the eternal, indestructible soul. For no matter what happens to you in this life, nothing can destroy your soul, your essence, your eternal nature. Our task is to hold that paradox, to be in two realities at once—like a stage actor.

The great actor totally experiences the full range of emotions of his character. The tears and laughter and everything in between are real and immediate, completely in the moment. Yet, at the same time, any actor knows that there is a sea of people watching the play. There are many human beings beyond the proscenium arch at the edge of the stage, who are actually in the same room.

In both the actor and the audience, there is an inner awareness of the dual reality of actors fully creating their characters' situation and at the same time being in a theatre which implies a different reality. As completely believable as the character becomes to the audience, that is not the whole story. Soon the actor will bow and go home to family and friends and enjoy soup and sleep. One story ends and another begins for all those present.

Can we also have an eye behind our daily eyes to remember the larger scene in which our life is cradled? As Shakespeare said in *The Tempest* (Act 4, Scene 1), "our little life is rounded with a sleep." As desperate and elevated and important as daily life becomes, soon we too will go to our eternal home for rest and renewal.

Holding these two realities in one mind, balancing these two co-existing worlds, allows us to be present in all that life gives us with ease and equanimity, accepting life on life's terms, living life with joy.

Certainly, we experience our grief, but we don't need to be personally destroyed or incapacitated by that grief, as we might be, if we forgot there are two worlds. We deny the power that the grief has over our indomitable soul. Yes, our loss is huge. Our life as we knew it, may be blown to bits, but simultaneously, we know that the soul will go on. The life force is strong within us. That is the power of the inner strength with which we can meet any limitation.

The spiritual path is one of paradox; practicing and getting expert at holding two seemingly opposite realities in the same place, at the same time. We don't choose one reality over the other. It is a "both-and" practice. "Yes—I am grieving" and "Yes—this loss won't destroy me nor harm the part of me that is eternal."

Not to hold both thoughts together can be deadening to you. Not to accept and embrace your grief, can make you feel out of touch and cold and closed off to the human situation. Not to remember the Truth of your soul's resilience makes your loss too heavy for the very cells to bear, and can push body and mind into a downward spiral of despair and hopelessness.

Balance within the paradox is the key. You can take turns—cry tears of blood, and then remember your soul's eternal life and wisdom and breathe again. Move back and forth like a seesaw—one side up and now the other one—up and down—as many times as you need. Sometimes you will come to a tenuous balance; hovering with your feet slightly off the ground on that emotional/spiritual seesaw. One day you will just know that this phase of the process has ended and you are on to another.

# SACRED PROCESS

## BUT HOW DO I GRIEVE?

Some may not need to ask this question because their emotions are so close to the surface. But if you find you require something to prime the pump, here are some suggestions:

1. Just being with friends can help you to heal through the presence of their love and support.
2. Talk it out—in person, on the phone, with a support group, to an individual therapist, in writing, through expressive art (drawing, clay, singing, writing etc.) And again, talk it out.
3. Reminisce. Tell or write stories of your memories.
4. Journal. This is a profound way express yourself and to make sense of your outer world and your inner experience. Some people feel that journaling is so powerful that it can by itself heal the heart.
5. Take some time to do nothing. Most employers will allow a period of leave after the loss of a significant person in your life. Yet eventually returning to a routine can help to ground you and re-orient you back to your life.
6. Put off major decisions like selling the house or giving away mementos.
7. Have quiet times. Shut off the media, computer, phone.
8. Review old pictures, slides, videos.
9. Cry, sleep, dream, record your dreams, feed yourself very well, walk, stretch.
10. Avoid alcohol and drugs as they keep you removed from your inner experience.

11. Take breaks with music, reading, movies, alone or with friends.

12. Allow someone to hold you if that feels comfortable to both of you.

13. Receive body work. A gentle soothing massage and energy work can help to release the sadness from the tissues in your body.

14. Use creative rituals to express feelings beyond words. One idea is to light a candle and pray for your loved one each month on the same day of their death for the first year then repeat that ritual on their yearly anniversary date.

15. Pray. Prayer is another way of talking, but to God this time. Prayer is a direct way to connect with your inner knowing and with the Divine.

16. Meditate or contemplate in silence. There are many meditation techniques. Find one that works for you and devote a portion of each day to its practice. It's a way to gently and consistently develop your eternal soul and provides peace and serenity for all your days. Scientific research has shown how any form of meditation can heal the brain from traumas. This practice actually creates new connective tissue in the brain.

17. Remember, above all to be gentle with yourself. The natural process of healing will unfold in its perfect time.

# CHAPTER 3

## The Soul Revealed

"What can be seen is temporary, but what
cannot be seen is eternal."

— 2 Corinthians 4:18

## Mark, My Teacher

As a child, I knew, by rote what happens to the body and the soul at death, but these concepts remained unreal and inaccessible to me. It wasn't until I had a direct experience with one of my greatest teachers that I truly understood the nature of the soul. His gift to me helped to bridge the world of matter and spirit, opened my spiritual awareness, and brought me peace and freedom from the cavernous fear of death. This amazing teacher appeared in a most unlikely package.

He is my second brother, Mark Anthony. My parents said they were embarrassed by the name they chose for their third child because Marc Antony was a colossal Roman warrior, and our Mark Anthony was a small tike who never grew taller than 4 feet. But, in truth, Mark was rightly named because he was actually a great warrior on the spiritual level.

I remember the day that Mom and Dad brought Markie home from the hospital. I was seven years old and so happy to greet my new baby brother. He was so tiny that through the next months my parents' concerns only grew. I overheard things like "breeched baby," that Mark was born feet first and was deprived of oxygen. He had a below-average birth weight and height, and Mom hadn't felt well all during her pregnancy with him; but I never knew why Markie was different.

I did, however, get clues from the neighbors. One little girl noticed that Mark and her brother were born about the same time, but her brother was walking and Markie was still lying in his crib until someone could pick him up. One day this neighbor girl taunted me and gloated that "her brother was better than mine." I had always been a child that others beat up because I didn't defend myself, but not on that day. On that particular day, I knocked that girl down and squished her like a bug. My loyalty to Mark rose up in me and that girl went home crying because she mocked innocent little Markie.

Another time, while having dinner for the first and last time at a certain peer's house, quite out of the blue in front of her whole family, my classmate said, "Your little brother is retarded, isn't he?" I had never heard that word used about him but I guessed she might be right. I said, "Yes, he is, but we don't call him retarded." After that meal, I raced home to bury my head and my tears in my pillow. I asked my father about it and Mom and Dad confirmed what I had suspected.

You see, back then, retardation wasn't a household word. I remember right around that time, there was a ground-breaking film that came out, the first of its kind, called *Charlie*. This was the first time Hollywood addressed the issue of retardation. It was glamorized, but at least the label was out of the closet. Shortly after that, the Kennedy family publicly spoke of their retarded daughter, Rosemary. Of course, we've come a long way in our understanding and speaking about all types of people with disabilities and for the most part, we no longer use hurtful labels. The term we use today is developmentally delayed.

I know my parents were ashamed to have a child with such a disability. I know they both blamed themselves. I'm sure there must have been some anger at God as well. I remember Markie and I being taken on a pilgrimage with my parents to St. Anne de Beaupre, a Catholic Church in Quebec known for miraculous healings. At the back of the church there was a large column filled with abandoned crutches, and other acknowledgements of answered prayers, but Markie never received the healing for which we prayed.

Mark remained tiny and would probably have failed to thrive, if it were not for the powerful love and determination of our mother. Right from infancy, Mark had great difficulty in eating and seemed to have no appetite for food. Mom would sit with Mark on her lap for hours getting him to take what small amount of food he would ingest. When he was very small, she fed him with an eye dropper. At every meal, Mark would fight Mom. He'd squirm on her lap and try to knock the food away, and he'd pinch the arm that held him still enough to get the food in his mouth. Sometimes he'd pinch so hard that Mom's arm would bleed. This went on three times a day for five years, but slowly Mark began not to resist living so very much. Somehow, he made peace with his life, as it was.

In later years, Mom shared with me her thoughts that perhaps if she hadn't tried so hard to get nutrition into Mark, he might have died. But how could she watch her baby starve to death? There could be no other choice for my mother.

It took several years to discover what was wrong with Mark. After the diagnosis was clear, our pediatrician advised my parent that they should place Mark in an institution. He felt that Mark's care took too much time and attention away from my middle brother who was only eighteen months older than Mark. And, of course, I lost my parents' care as well. I was expected to be mature and not need them, but I did need them. Finally, when Mark was five years old, they agreed.

It was a very difficult decision for my parents to remove their child from our home. It was a decision that took years to make. We children were precious to our parents regardless of our abilities or disabilities. I know that in recent times, there is a different attitude about group homes for children with disabilities but in the early 1960s, there remained a stigma derived from centuries of institutional conditions that ranged from inefficient to barbaric.

Our parents eventually placed Mark in the State Institution at Perrysburg, NY. It was a cavernous, former tuberculosis recovery hospital. Located just an hour from our home, yet it was in an area I had never seen before it became Mark's new home. I remember how very hard it was to say goodbye to Mark when we took him to Perrysburg. It never got much easier.

Sunday afternoons became reserved for visits and outings with Markie. Even though Mark never talked, he knew that Sundays were his time with us. The attendants said that each Sunday, he would sit in the hall waiting for Mom to come. We'd visit with him there, or take him out to a park or sometimes bring him home. We all loved being together with him. Being apart was hard and our hearts broke to hear Mark mournfully cry each time we left him in his ward at the end of our visit.

Being a sibling of a disabled child can be confusing and difficult. As my parents were ashamed and blamed themselves for having such a child, I took on the shame as well. My childhood needs always seemed less important than those of the child with special needs. I'm sure I felt guilty for even asking for what I wanted in the face of the enormous time and attention Mark needed, so mostly, I didn't ask.

In such a situation, any sibling can slip into an adult role. Children may cope by unconsciously discerning their niche and becoming valuable to the family by doing whatever they can to help out, remaining as self-sufficient as possible, so as not to make more problems for the already over-taxed parents.

Despite all that, it was easy to love Mark's unique and joyful personality. He seemed to be endlessly curious like toddlers can be, and he was always getting into mischief in his exploring. Our Markie was forever a sweet child with an infectious laugh and he loved to hear Chip play the harmonica. Chip would nestle on the couch and start playing his free-form music and Mark would stop whatever he was doing and make a bee-line, crawling and climbing onto the couch, placing his head on Chip's lap and remaining unusually still, mesmerized by those sounds. It was a touching sight from such a rambunctious child.

## The Teaching

I have said that Mark was one of my great teachers. One February night, a night of freezing dampness when it seemed the winter would last forever, Mom called me home. Markie lay dying in the hospital. At twenty-three years old, he had outlived the predictions of his life expectancy and his body was giving out. His kidneys were failing. So we three, Mom, Chip, and I began the round-the-clock hospital vigil that would change my life forever.

What was most noticeable about Mark in the hospital bed was how very much his spine was twisted. The pillows were positioned to prop his left leg over to the right and his shoulders were facing the left. Premature osteoporosis imprinted a corkscrew on his skeleton. He couldn't lay flat.

For days and nights we were with Mark at his bedside. When we spoke to him, he often opened his eyes in response. We barely left his side, but one night around three a.m., exhaustion swept over us and the nurse encouraged us to go down the hall to the waiting room where we could stretch out on couches and chairs. She assured us she would keep watch with Mark and call us when it was time. Just as we were falling into that relaxed level of sleep, the nurse called us. "Hurry. He's going."

Chip shot up first and ran to Markie's side. I wanted to run, too, but I stayed next to Mom and half supported-carried her as she couldn't run because of an old injury. We got there in time. Through his tears, Chip cried out, "Markie." Mom tenderly advised, "No, no, don't call him back." I marveled at how she knew things about dying. I was bewildered and scared and so grateful Mom was there with us. Of course, she had assisted her father and mother and two brothers and my father in their dying process, so she knew what to expect. I wondered if I would ever be knowledgeable about such a mystery, so that I could be of help to Mom, when her end-day would come.

And then, the teaching came.

As I held Mark's left hand, Chip on his right, Mom stroking Mark's head, I was aware of the flow of life in his hand. His labored breathing stopped with one last exhale, and in an instant, there was no life in his hand. One second there was life—then no life. I felt that there was something that went somewhere. Some part of him that had been present was gone. I felt it leave—his essence, his energy, his soul, his light-being. I saw him rise out of the top of his head and hover above his body and behind his head. I perceived his soul, clearly, unmistakably present in the air. It was whole and simply some place other than in his body.

I was amazed. I had never witnessed anything like this. My perceiving came differently than through my five senses. In a pause in time, I experienced a type of feeling-sight, an airy, filmy image that I felt-saw in the room and that registered in my own being. Although it was unusual, I knew it was real, more real than anything else.

And then I saw the transfiguration of what remained as his body.

His body was completely straight! How did it happen? Did his body just relax deeply, I wondered? He was no longer twisted. He was lying absolutely flat on his back, an impossible position seconds before. Then I noticed his face! Throughout his life, Mark always had a look that revealed his disability. Anyone looking at him could tell that he was delayed. But as I looked at him now, that previously distorted countenance was gone! In death he was transformed, and his face shone with a pure and angelic radiance.

Here was the profound teaching Mark showed me about our eternal and immortal soul. Any words I had heard about death and the soul were just intellectual concepts until I experienced his death and saw that we are more than a body. Our soul inhabits and fills out our flesh and then, when our body is left without that energy, the body simply goes limp and can be discarded. Our body is no longer necessary because our soul goes on without it. Our soul is bigger than when we came into the world. It has been filled up with a lifetime of learning and growth. Hopefully, our soul has deepened with compassion and understanding and awareness of the Truth of our amazing path through this world and beyond. Our only purpose here on earth is to love, and the more we love, the brighter our inner light becomes.

Mark was freed not only from life. He was freed from this particular role that he'd accepted to play in this lifetime, like an actor taking off his makeup and costume. The "delayed" part was layered on top of who he really was. That part was lifted, gone, like a mask removed. What remained was a beautiful little boy, with a look of peace and dignity on his face. This miraculous transformation of Mark's soul and body confirmed the truth for me that he was much more than a limited, finite individual.

My brother's life summons this inquiry, "Can we begin to see with new eyes all the souls in this world as living inside their masks?" We all have a mask that we will eventually leave behind. It's a mask of our unique face and personality which never has and never will be repeated again. But the very core of us remains for all eternity as does Mark's. He chose to come into this life simply to receive and give love. His very being was a gift to all of us.

## Thoughts on the Soul

What really does happen to us when we die? Where does our soul go?

My interest heightened and I pondered these questions after a series of deaths in my family. I deeply yearned to know the answer, fearing the inevitable day when I would be standing alone at the bedside of my dying loved one or, perhaps, I'd be the one in that bed.

Our soul can choose to return directly to the Light, back to the Source. It can let go of any earthly attachments knowing it has completed its walk. The soul is free of the body and any and all physical suffering. The chapter is complete. So death must be like soaring, like the ethereal hawks as they spread their wings and are lifted by the wind. They are carried effortlessly, like one long exhale. We come into this world with an inhale and as we leave, we take one last exhale. It's good to remember that the final exhale on earth is the beginning of our soaring flight in the world of Spirit.

The breath that breathes us through all our life is Spirit within us, and that same Spirit carries us forth on the ongoing journey of our soul's development. We are never alone.

We know that just because the hawk glides far and eventually out of our sight, he hasn't disappeared. He continues on and so does our soul. He is not lost and neither are we. He is just beyond our sight, still very real and present wherever he is. And so it is with our soul.

As a Catholic I was taught that our faith affirms life beyond death, that our soul is eternal and immortal. In later years, I found agreement with this teaching not only in Christianity but throughout the world religions.

The following are quotations from several world religions as mentioned in *How Different Religions View Death and Afterlife*, edited by Christopher Jay Johnson, PhD. and Marsha G. McGee, PhD. with page references.

**Native American**—Most Native American people have a well-developed concept of the soul. They believe that the human soul is preexistent, meaning that it existed before birth, and that souls come from the gods or Great Spirit. Coming from the gods makes the soul supernatural but also sensual, connected to the body through the senses as well as the intellect. (See Ake Hultkrantz, *Soul and Native Americans.*)

**Judaism**—"The Lord God formed man of dust from the ground and breathed into his nostrils the breath of life and man became a living soul." Genesis 2:7

"May the soul be bound up in the bonds of eternal life." (Paraphrased from 1 Samuel 25:29 customary to be used on Jewish headstones.) (Johnson & McGee, p. 159).

**Hinduism**—The *Upanishads* [Hindu sacred scripture] reveal that the essence of each human being is the imperishable Self or soul, which does not die with the body...The human "soul" (or atman) is described as intangible, indestructible, and unbound...[It] is the 'true (divine) nature' of the person which persists after the death of the body." (*Brihadaranyaka Upanishad* 3.9.26). (Johnson & McGee, p. 114).

**Islam**—Immediately after the death of an individual "the soul, now separated from the body, embarks on a journey." *Qur'an.* (Johnson & McGee, p. 138).

**Buddhism**—The mind does continue—so does love and compassion and insight into the nature of things. "Consciousness itself, described as an entity of clarity and knowing, retreats from the sense organs, finally gathering at the center of the heart before departing the body."(Johnson & McGee, p. 55).

**Zoroastrianism**—"The body is mortal, [but] the soul is eternal. Do good deeds for the soul... [as] the spiritual realm is what matters, not the material world." (*Chidag Handarz i Poryotkeshan*, 1.55 – from the 9th century Pahlavi book). (Johnson & McGee, p. 257).

## SOUL SONG

What fills you from chest to back
from head to foot?
It is not air or only tissues and blood.
What fills you is Light,
Light that exists in the spaces and in the matter of all that
is you.
Light that is stronger than anything on earth.
Loving Light that heals, harmonizes, uplifts and
transcends.

You will know the Light that you are
on that final day of your earthly walk.
You will know the eternal magnificence of yourself as soul.
Your True Self will rise, soaring like the phoenix
from the ashes left behind.

Why wait until death to know your true and eternal Self?
All the Light that you will ever be is fully within you now.
Light is who you are
who you have been,
    are now,
      will be,
        forever more.

Welcome now the inevitability of your death
so that you can live free as the eternal you right now;
so that you can live every day as if you had all eternity.
You do.
Life, Life, Life is the song your heart is waiting to sing.

# SACRED PROCESS

## YOU ARE A SOUL

"The purpose of our life on earth is to help our soul to grow. When we leave earth all we take with us is what we have become."

Stella Terrill Mann

Soul is the total of our experiences gathered throughout the ages including our conscious and subconscious memories. It is our accumulation of all we have learned. It is who we really are for all eternity.

1. Looking back over your life, make a list of all the happenings that you feel made you a bigger, greater, expanded soul. For example, jot down times when you:
   * overcame adversity
   * chose the right road rather than the negative path
   * aligned yourself with and lived from spiritual principles
2. Review your list and celebrate the greater "you" you have created yourself to be.
3. Soul Skills are any part of life, learning and practice that make us larger, magnanimous beings. They include things such as generosity, faith, love, compassion, forgiveness, service, wisdom and discernment, equanimity, moral conscience, appreciation of beauty, courage to speak your truth, imagination, optimism, and embracing the negative attributes or shadow self as a part of ourselves that we haven't previously been able to accept.

Recall and write down the experiences in your life that increased the skills of your soul.
For example, courage to speak your truth.

Has it become easier for you to speak your truth as you've grown older?
Has practice made you more compassionate in choosing your words?
If so, what helped you to strengthen this soul ability?

4. Continue this type of inquiry for all of your soul skills.
5. To develop your soul: Love, Love, Love.
   Love life in all its variety and be eternally curious about it.
   Love your memories that recall times of joy, harmony and peace.
   Love people. As you give and receive love your quality of love will deepen and the energy of your love will expand. Tears of gratitude may flow as your heart grows in its capacity to give and receive even more love. Then life truly becomes exquisite and delicious.

# CHAPTER 4

## Expanding Our Thinking

"I think my life began with waking up and
loving my mother's face."

— GEORGE ELIOT

## Anna Marie

WHAT IS IT like to step across a threshold and see there before
you all your relatives and friends, even some you knew from
grade school, cheering in unison as you enter? They all
exclaim at once, "Surprise!" like a flash exploding and forever freezing this moment in memory.

It was the start of Mom's surprise seventieth birthday
brunch. Her delight in this first surprise party of her life
combined with mild shock as Mom reeled, amazed by all the
people assembled in that one room. The shock of it seemed
to take her breath away. She sat on the couch through
most of the party, happy and engaged, but uncharacteristically sedentary, which surprised me. Mom whispered to me
later during the party, that she was having some medical
tests at the beginning of the next week. I knew she hadn't
been feeling at all well for quite a while—indigestion, we
thought at first.

Can you imagine *our* surprise when later that week, Mom's
doctor shared his findings: our mother had stomach cancer

and needed an operation to remove the tumor. We waited outside the operating room, praying that this surgery would heal her. Can you imagine our shock when the surgeon reported that he couldn't get all of the cancer, even after removing 90% of her stomach? I fell into freeze frame numbness as he continued that she had limited time left to live.

No…No…No…No…

Who was this woman beyond her role as my mother?

"Five foot two, eyes of blue…" I always thought of Mom when I heard this flapper song from the era in which she was born. The only daughter with three brothers she was born of immigrant parents twelve years before the Great Depression into a home of poverty and alcoholism. Anna Marie made a difficult choice when she decided to leave school and abandon her love of learning after her sophomore year in high school. She did this in order to find work to support her family. She spent her life working hard and assuming the broad shoulders of responsibility.

My Mom didn't speak much of those hard times. She didn't like to dwell in the past, but she did mention that there was a visiting social worker who came to their home in her early years. This woman's care and concern and presence was a singular light in a sea of darkness and made such a lasting impression that Mom wanted to become a social worker. She always held this dream in her heart, but it was never realized. The needs of her loved ones always took precedence in my Mom's choices.

As a young woman she was quite a looker. She dressed with style and flair. No wonder she attracted movie-star handsome Leonard, nine years her senior. She said the age difference never mattered because he was so youthful and she was very mature.

They both desired to transform their difficult early years into a life and home filled with love, joy, and prosperity, based on sound practices and principles. Through their powerful intention, they devoted themselves to creating an environment that would support their children by giving them all the opportunities they never had. Providing a good education was highest on their list.

Because of their intention to provide, lack or limitation wasn't in our vocabulary. My mother was a master at handling the single pay check that Dad brought home to her from his work as a barber. Somehow she made the money stretch to cover all that we needed including private high schools for my brother and me, as well as savings. Nothing was extravagant but I never heard that easy excuse that we "couldn't afford" something. I realize now that Mom's frugal and assertive style made it all work. She didn't spend a lot on herself, but as in all things, it was her joy to give to her family.

Mom said that her life with my father was the best time of her life and yet her life was hard. They so wanted a child, but after ten years of trying to get pregnant, they finally surrendered to the possibility that they might never give birth to one. Finally, I came along. Mom said in her spicy way, "After our first child, it seemed that every time Dad dropped his pants I became pregnant." Then there were two miscarriages and one was far enough along for them to know it was a boy. Dad got the chance to see that little boy and hold it and said the infant resembled him.

Then came my precious brother, five and a half years after me. He was the happiest, most contented child. He reminded everyone of the Gerber baby with a sweet, round face, smiling and cooing most of the time. Dad finally got his little boy! They nick-named him Chip, "Chip off the old block."

Then came our little brother, Mark. Mom felt she was probably too old to have had him, but he came, nonetheless, one and half years after Chip. Mom told me she felt so happy and healthy during her pregnancy with Chip, but experienced such a contrast when she carried Mark. She didn't feel well during her whole pregnancy. Mark was difficult, difficult to feed, to nurture, to keep alive. Eventually, as I've already shared, we learned he was severely mentally disabled.

Can you imagine what it's like to have a child and feel in your heart that something is not right, but you must wait in limbo until the baby is a little older in order to have your worst suspicions confirmed? How long was that waiting time? Months, more than a year until the doctor could make a definitive diagnosis. What did Dad and Mom do during that time of agony? I know Mom did her best to nurture Mark and help him thrive. Even after the diagnosis, they continued to try to care for him and kept Mark at home with us for his first five years.

When Mark was placed in an institution, we found to our horror, that some parents abandoned their child to a life of care by the hospital staff. My mother would never do that. My mother was a grounded and strong advocate for Mark, especially in the face of any injustice. At one point, Mark had a broken leg and the staff couldn't say how it happened. Mom got to the bottom of it and discovered it was a male aide who pulled Mark up by one of his arms and then crashed Mark down on his leg so hard that Mark's leg broke. Mom pressed charges and the man was fired. She was fearless in her ability to fight for what was right, and to win.

She had a strong will to achieve, keen mental clarity, a sense of humor, intelligence, as well as worldly smarts, resourcefulness, high principles and tenacity. I believe because of her thwarted potential, her frustration would sometimes turn to anger. She expected her children to be all she would never be. She was so tuned into us that I sometimes felt she even knew my thoughts. Nothing escaped her, yet we always knew we were intensely loved.

After Dad and Mark died and Chip and I were each married off and out in the world, it seemed there might finally be a time for Mom's own peace and happiness. She revisited one of her personal dreams. She decided to get her GED, her high school equivalency diploma. It had been years since she was in school and studied, but with the help of our generous neighbor, Evelyn, coaching her in English skills, Mom achieved her goal. It was a great and proud day for her to complete the education which she had curtailed so long ago to care for her family instead. And then only a couple of years after this triumph, the diagnosis of cancer and a death sentence.

NO---------------Not her---------------Not now----------------

The waiting room listed like a ship and the walls seemed to vomit green. A distorted "fun-house" mirror became the lens I peered through, as we sat with Mom and heard the surgeon tell her of their treatment plan for killing off the defective cells, and that despite the treatment, she didn't have long to live.

I couldn't absorb this information, so I set about to do what I could to help Mom heal. I took her to a Bernie Siegel workshop after reading his groundbreaking book, *Love, Medicine and Miracles.* We learned about our rights as patients. We didn't have to buy into anyone's prediction, not even a doctor's, telling us when we will die. That's playing God. No one can tell you when you will die. Your end time is a sacred contract between you and God and so is your dying process. We were told that death is a great mystery. Each death is unique and has the profound ability to create closure specifically designed for the final spiritual needs of that individual.

I don't know if Mom was thinking these thoughts when she confided in me that, "Of course, suicide is not an option for us." I know our family religion forbids suicide, and my mother would abide by those revered teachings. She would also find the courage to trust and surrender to the dying process she was entering. Her statement closed the option of assisted suicide and I was spared that particular turmoil of family members who are asked to assist a dying loved one, thereby violating the laws at that time.

It was my experience with Mom that clarified my feelings about assisted suicide. During those two and a half years from her birthday party until her death: witnessing her surgery, chemotherapy, disintegration of her body, her waiting and boredom, and the pain that eventually necessitated a morphine drip and more, I could firmly agree with her decision that suicide would never be an option for us.

Such a conviction does not preclude the need for expert palliative care to ease the pain so the person can relax and be present to their dying process. If one chooses, there can be a signed directive, a living will, to ensure that the doctor will not resuscitate, nor attach the patient to life support, nor insert a feeding tube when the person can no longer eat. These directives would not interfere with the natural dying process.

Perhaps your journey on this earth is teaching you to trust and honor life with increasing ease and grace, to surrender more often to life on life's terms. Therefore, it makes good sense to choose going through the dying process in a natural way so that your unique experience of dying will assist your soul's growth. Spiritual surrender expands your inner core of being.

A friend confided in me her experience of sharing the end-time with her father. She loved her father, but they had had a rocky relationship all her life. When, in his final weeks, he reverted to his pattern of verbally abusing her, she seriously thought of not seeing him anymore and allowing him to die without her. Then, somehow, he changed and found it within himself to tell her how much he really loved her. This sincere connection and expression was what she'd waited for all her life. Perhaps it was the dying process that changed this man and allowed him to get to the truth of his love for his daughter. In the cavernous reality of death, many of us finally get with the program, and see the light and put things into perspective. If my friend's father had chosen to end his life before his natural time came because he feared the pain or some other aspect of the process, both he and his daughter would have been deprived of the healing they both finally experienced.

Our prayers and intentions for healing may or may not result in healing of the body. The healing we pray for may occur in healing the eternal soul—that carries on forever. That healing is arguably more important and certainly longer lasting than the healing of the body.

I had the great privilege of hearing Dr. Elisabeth Kubler-Ross speak about her mother's dying. Elisabeth's mother was very active and healthy when she spoke with Elisabeth asking her to assist her in suicide, if she should become incapacitated. Elisabeth told her mother that she could not agree to do that, given her oath as a doctor and all that she had stood for in her life's work. Besides, Elisabeth thought it was strange that her mother would even bring up such a request to be euthanized, since she was so vitally alive.

However, two weeks later Elisabeth's mother suffered a stroke and was in a totally dependent state for the next four years until she died. Elisabeth would not help her mother to circumvent her natural process. Her mother had always been a very independent person and had a difficult time accepting any assistance. She would always rather do it herself. Elisabeth realized that as a result of the stroke, her mother now had to accept assistance all the time for every part of her life and care. Perhaps her mother had to go through this experience in order to heal that part of her that had been so out of balance. She had four years to make up for a life time of not being able to ask for help. It wasn't easy for either of them, but finally, Elisabeth came to an understanding that made sense to her.

Our being wants balance and wholeness and will use every last breath to bring that healing to us. There is Divine Order and compassionate ever-present love from God even in the end-times. My final days with my Mother also taught me many things, and I know she healed into her dying as well.

## Regarding Suicide

It is important to speak about suicide because so many people have been touched by it. When you know a person who has committed suicide, if you're like me, you probably remember them very vividly. Each person who I knew who took his or her own life has left an indelible mark on my heart. The choice to end one's own life is so much the antithesis of our all abiding internal "will to live" that we sense how much pain the person must have suffered to commit such an act.

Depression is a mental illness and like the illness of cancer, depression can kill. Even though the final actions of suicide are often filled with rage, desperation, violence and lack of judgment, I do know this violation is not who the person really is in their essence.

We don't know the purpose for anyone's life and death but we know they are light-filled spiritual beings, and through death they move back to the spirit realm, to resolve any issues that were not settled during their earthly walk. Every soul is held responsible for its actions and simultaneously held in deep, unconditional love and forgiveness.

We know that the survivors of a suicide often blame themselves, but there is no blame here. Mothers, fathers, sisters, brothers, spouses, children, other relatives, counselors, friends, all who knew the individual did the best they could. The person's choice outweighed theirs. There is no blame on the ones who remain. No more could have been done.

## A Strong Constitution

My mother would always proudly cluck, "I've never been sick a day in my life. I don't get colds or flu, and I never have any back pain, like so many women complain about. I have a cast iron stomach." She enjoyed drinking black boiler pot coffee, throughout the day. She never seemed to need to rest while working in the house all day, though she did sit down for meals.

My mom wasn't ever cold, keeping the thermostat at 60 degrees even in Buffalo winters. "Just put on another sweater," was her remark to those of us with lesser body heat.

Yes, my Mother had a great, strong constitution, so you can imagine the shock and disbelief of all of us when, at seventy years old, this indomitable force received the news that she had cancer. This mighty five-foot-two inch power-house was dead in a fleeting two years. How could it be? Such an early and rapid death didn't make sense. What about that strong constitution?

I have come to learn that people often label strong constitutions as "healthy" because they seem to be impervious to outside forces. They can will their way through weakness, tiredness, fear, and deadlines, muscling through pretty much everything like the Ever Ready Bunny who keeps on going, or our popular culture super heroes who are invincible.

Do we celebrate this heroic type as another expression of our collective denial of the natural ebb and flow of life itself? Within the balance of life, every hill has a valley just as every stretched muscle must also contract. Perhaps our values are off center regarding the true health of the indomitable. For example, in the British 1948 film, *The Red Shoes,* when the dancer put on the magical dancing shoes she couldn't stop dancing until she died. Like that when we can't stop, rest, change gears and surrender to what is, but must always go full speed ahead, lack of balance will eventually claim its due.

So I've come to see the potential of a weaker constitution's ability to come back to health and balance more often because, a weaker constitution *needs* to find balance more often. Every draft, every spicy meal, every late night binge wreaks havoc on the delicate constitution.

When you can't go on because you have a cold at the beginning of the change of seasons in autumn, perhaps it's a way that your body demands and gets its rest, releasing toxins, and re-balancing to begin again fresh and renewed. And when we "can't" go on, when we must surrender, is that really something to be ashamed of, or is it just another marker along the bumpy landscape of life? We are invited to look more deeply and carefully at what is health and who is really healthy.

## Forgiveness

Never being one to complain, the pain and discomfort in her stomach must have been intense for Mom to see her doctor about it initially.

At this time, at sixty-five and on Medicare, her health care provider was assigned by an HMO. Her new doctor was quite young and didn't know her. He interpreted her complaints and symptoms as the stereotype of a lonely old woman wanting some attention. By not hearing her, not believing her when she first brought her pain to him, he wasted those irreplaceable months of an early diagnosis, and helped to seal her fate.

After her surgery, however, her doctor became devoted to her. He made himself always available to her and even made house calls. He seemed to be more like her son. And she came to rely on his judgment and appreciate his care and their special relationship. After surgery, he apologized to her, saying that he hadn't really listened to her when she first came to him, and if he had heard her, it could've made a difference in the outcome. Receiving this admission, my mother knew that she could sue him, but she told me she didn't want to spend her final days in a legal battle. Instead, she forgave him. He told her he would always remember her. She would be with him in his work, and he promised to remember the lesson she taught him: to listen so as to truly hear. Somehow, in this cosmic dance of life and death, both doctor and woman rose to their innate magnificence.

## Last Seasons

Have you ever wondered where and how you'd like to spend the last winter of your life, if you are given the chance?

Without question, although none of us was sure that it would be her last winter, my mother chose to be near the beach with me in Miami. She so loved the ocean and walking on the beach and I was happy to have her with me. Mom and her significant other, Bob Crouse, came to live with me in

November. Mom was feeling fairly well that winter. Since the removal of most of her stomach, she was thin and, I thought, very beautiful and chic in her new physical form.

By March, however, we knew she'd have to return to her doctors in Buffalo. She was in pain again as her cancer had continued to grow and spread to her ovary. However, she expressed a last wish to take me on a weekend cruise out of Miami. I had never taken a cruise during all the years I had lived in that cruise capital. Mom wanted her children to enjoy all the good that there was to experience. And of course, this would be our last trip and I knew she meant it to be a special memory for us.

During the days, we did the usual sunning, sightseeing on the land, and sitting with our table of others at dinner. Mom shared with me that she was amazed that these people had no idea how ill she really was. She might mention her condition to one of the table-mates, but she seemed to be so happy to be there, so lit from within at times, that they never really got the significance of her words.

But the nights were difficult. Mom couldn't lay down flat. She had to sit up because of the reflux occurring. I spent most of the nights holding her, cradling her in my arms, silently praying that she'd get through the night. The sound of her choking, laboring for breath, trying to clear, this terrifying sound of her body rejecting the food, rejecting life, that sound would not be stopped. It is a sound that haunted me for a long, long time.

Finally, by April, we knew it was time for her to make her last trip home. She needed her doctors and to be in Hospice care, and she wanted to be in her own home. I don't know if we really understand how important familiar surroundings can be to someone, especially at this stage. Perhaps it's like a bird that has taken leaves and small branches in her beak, almost one at a time, laying them carefully to form a nest—a place of comfort and safety and rest, for the important birth of the new life that is coming. Can we understand the hours and years of nesting that a person does, layering memory and safety, hollowing out the space in her own home to nestle into. It's the best place to be.

I was not at all ready to let her go "gentle into that good night." I claimed my mission and my desire, to care for her to the best of my ability. For the next six months, I used vacation time to travel home to care for her ten days each month. Thankfully, Bob was able to be with her the rest of the time, and Hospice gave thoughtful care as well.

Then, in October, I took an unpaid, indefinite leave of absence from a family service agency where I held a position as a licensed clinical social worker. I was grateful that they held my position for me, but I would have left, even if they hadn't. My mother needed me and I needed her. More than twenty years after my father slipped away when I wasn't present, I decided I would not miss another parent's leaving. I vowed in my heart to be fully present and to help her in any way that I could. I refused to be frightened or intimidated or deterred by death. I would look death in the face and survive.

Our prayers, up to this point, were filled with our deepest desire for my Mother's complete recovery, that she be restored to a fullness of life, free of illness. But now, although that yearning for total life was still present, there was a part of us that was beginning to accept the inevitability of her death. And yet, it felt too soon to pray for an easy death, because there was still hope. Miracles were still possible.

I remembered Dr. Elisabeth Kubler-Ross strongly cautioning that no one has the right to erase a patient's or family's hope. Even in the face of extreme debilitation, we have a right to continue to hope for a cure for as long as we choose. In fact, most people who wish to be euthanized by assisted suicide, state that hopelessness is the biggest reason for their decision, not pain, as one might expect. Hope is a sacred right. One moment you might have hope for a cure and in the next moment there is no hope. This is a natural progression toward acceptance. If the person continues to move toward death, it will become obvious to that person and to their family. As in all of life, a healthy balance needs to be found between pulling the rug of hope out from under a person and squelching the reality of the coming of their end times.

At the same time I have witnessed denial of the reality of dying. Unexpressed truth and feelings sit like an elephant in the middle of your living room. Everyone is aware of this huge presence, but if no one talks about it, it is a great disservice to the person dying as well as to those around him or her. We are called to listen deeply to the hints of what the person needs. Listen more than talk, ask questions rather than make assumptions. Accept where the dying person is and respond accordingly.

When I found myself in this situation, I wondered how to pray, and what to pray for? What was my desire for Mom at this point? What were her wishes? What authentic language could I use to truly reflect a positive possibility at this particular time in her illness?

I mentioned two authors whose books helped us both on this journey: Dr. Bernie Siegel, and Dr. Elisabeth Kubler-Ross. Have you had times in your life when it seemed that messages from the Divine simply land in your lap right when you need them? I don't remember how I came to have this next book, but its presence and messages were merciful to us. It infused our "autumn days" with compassionate guidance and support. Stephen Levine's, *Who Dies: An Investigation of Consciously Living and Consciously Dying*, became our text. Stephen Levine is a poet and teacher of meditation and healing techniques, and a renowned writer on death and dying. Here I found profound ideas and Mom was completely open to discussing and embracing many of the practices that the book suggested.

Of course, there were many "to-do's" even in these final months that seemed to take much of our day: Hospice visits, bathing, feeding and medication, etc. So my mother and I chose to have our prayer time at five p.m. each night. We began with the rosary and when that became too long and tiring for Mom, we chose shorter prayers. Five p.m. became our sacred time. We didn't allow other distractions, no phone calls, no other appointments or "things to do." This was our special time with each other and with God. After our prayers, I read a chapter from Levine's book to Mom and the ideas primed and deepened our discussions about dying and pain and unfinished business. It allowed both of us closure in various areas of our lives. I offer some of them for you to use in any way that speaks to you.

The first topic was "healing". My original understanding of healing was limited in its scope. I saw healing as a return to complete and total wellness through the removal of the illness. But Levine made a distinction between "a cure" and "healing." A cure is moving totally beyond physical illness, but healing is much broader. Healing is coming to a wholeness in all parts of the being, not only physically but mentally, emotionally, and spiritually, as well. Healing is ultimately moving up higher in consciousness, coming to know who you truly are, and clarifying your relationship with God and with all of Life, regardless of whether you have an illness or not.

So along with our prayers for a cure, Mom and I also now prayed for deep and transformational healing. Our prayers had a new clarity, truth and hope. We embraced the reality of Mom's situation by accepting the presence of the illness and knowing that even in the midst of it all, we could pray for and claim a real and everlasting healing.

This broadened the meaning of hope as well. Even though accepting her terminal illness, Mom had hope in many areas. She hoped to have her financial affairs in order and to make sure her house sold so my brother and I could move on more easily. She spoke with us about dividing up her possessions according to our wishes so that we could carry out those decisions more easily in her absence. She had seen too many families fighting and breaking apart over possessions and didn't want our relationship to be harmed in that way. I didn't know then, but realized later that she wanted to see her only grandchild again before she died. I know she wanted to remain at home and die with her children around her. And I learned that my mother also wanted to more deeply understand her own spiritual connection to dying and death. All of these goals supported and sustained her sense of hope even when she released her hope for a cure.

These two months were very valuable time. Every minute up to the final breath is life and can be and should be held in that context. We have a choice to live fully until we die. There is divine potential in every moment of life for cures, for healing, for resolving the past, for paving the way for the new in relationships, for growth of the soul, and so much more than what we know. And these end-times are perhaps full of even more possibilities than the fleeting moments of ordinary daily life. Because of the illness, there is an urgency created that demands your attention on the things that matter the most. Because of the illness, there is less pull from the world, no more occupation, fewer "to-do" lists. Focusing on what is really important to you becomes more obvious. Without other distractions, and with death so close, most can center on what's essential and crucial to them. And in that empty and fertile landscape, healing can occur.

## Forgiveness Again

Mom and I also spent time on a universal ingredient of healing that is taught by every religion of the world and in all spiritual disciplines: the practice of forgiveness. Of course, we all make mistakes, but we all have the possibility to grow from our mistakes. Mistakes are such a common occurrence that when Peter came to Jesus and asked, "Lord, if another member of the church sins against me, how often should I forgive? As many as seven times?" Peter was thinking that seven times would be generous enough. Jesus replied, "Not seven times, but I tell you, seventy times seven" (Matthew 18:21–22). Jesus meant keep on forgiving, as long as there is more to forgive.

Certainly, my Mother practiced confessing her "sins" or mistakes in the context of her religion. She appreciated the opportunity of confession, and would tell me, "I always feel so much better after confession. I feel like a big weight is lifted from me." She did seem lighter and full of peace at those times. Here was a spiritual practice that she used that worked for her.

Something quite profound happened in our relationship when Mom asked me for my forgiveness for those times, those behaviors, those mistakes that she had made. She expressed her remorse in clear and quiet tones. I had never before heard her admit her mistakes and ask for forgiveness so directly. To witness someone take responsibility for harm done is a deep blessing and this communion between us has made all the difference to me then and ever since. Something shifted, something healed between us as that admission, that request was spoken and heard.

I did forgive her. There was no hesitation in that moment. To receive that gift, to hear her honesty, her vulnerability, allowed us to be more than mother and daughter. We became woman to woman, soul to soul. This expression transcended separation. We opened heart to heart. She took the chance in that moment to be courageous and real and blessed us both. I experienced dignity and honor, as she released regrets.

Gravesites are littered with tears of regret from both the living and the dead. "If only," the two saddest words in the world, echo through those rows of monuments. What "could have been done," "should have been done," actions that were never taken, feelings that never got expressed, take up our mental-emotional space and keep us stuck in the past.

I suffered for decades with deep regret for not being with my father at the time of his death. So I told Mom that I really wanted to be with her when she died, and I wondered if she wanted me to be with her at her time of death. She said, yes, if it worked out for me to be present, she did want me there. This allowed me to feel the peace of our agreement and our human plan. I knew the situation could change, but at least we expressed what we needed, what we wanted.

Ask your loved ones your questions. Tell them the important things, perhaps the most important, "I love you." And also be kind and wise. You might not want to bring up a topic at this stage that would hurt or upset them needlessly, just to get it off your chest. To ask and to give forgiveness allows for a fullness of peace to be in both of you. And isn't it peace that we ultimately wish for our loved ones?

## TO FORGIVE

Lying on my hard bed of judgments
ruins my sleep.
At each turn I feel the jab of
this one's humiliations, that one's stab in my back.
Nothing helps to smooth the lumps and bumps protruding
from thoughts under the sheets.

In my nightmare I hang off a cliff
dangling from one lone branch.
I cannot ascend to the ledge above,
neither will I allow myself to let go,
to plummet to my certain death
on the jagged boulders so far below.

Yet in my heart of hearts, I know I am safe beyond all
appearances.

Finally, with faith, I let go.
I let go of the hurt,
of holding on to the wish that it might be other than what
it is.
I choose to forgive.
I bless the ones who have taken away my grounding,
the ones who have made life an agonizing trial,
and I see the good I have created from this disarray
from this dust.

So in that leap to free-fall freedom,
releasing myself from the hanging hook of going nowhere
fast,
I wake in a soft bed of down comfort
under me, over me, cradling me
in fresh, sweet peace.
This is the blessed alchemy of forgiveness.

## Taking Care of the Caregiver

My intention to be fully present for Mom during this crucial time in her life meant that I must give total attention. A dying person's needs can be all consuming. They grow in scope and detail as the patient continues to lose strength and hold on life. Caregiving is a 24/7 job. I surrendered to doing everything that was needed. I kept details in mind so I could be vigilant in Mom's care. I wanted her to have the best possible quality of care and life for whatever time she had left. She and her needs became my total focus. I remarked in my journal, on September 19, 1988, when I was still "commuting" from my life in Miami to see her monthly in Buffalo:

This is all so time consuming. My attention is so much on her and trying to be of help that it's very hard to have a full life of my own. I feel that my life is on hold. I am waiting to live. I don't want to be like that, but if I make plans, I feel I won't be available to help her, so I wait, or feel guilty sometimes if I forget her or miss an opportunity to be of help. I am constantly thinking, when will I go back to see her? I wish I could be living more moment to moment, taking it one day at a time.

It's easy to be overwhelmed with caring for a loved one. Their needs are great, immediate and often urgent, and our needs can seem so puny compared to what our loved one is experiencing. We may put our needs, our life, on hold as we give everything to our loved one. Of course, this total concern at the expense of our own life, is not healthy. I knew this, yet I was pulled to immerse myself in her situation, especially when I returned to Buffalo. I wanted to go as deeply as I could into this experience with her. At the same time, I was conscious of my need for some sense of balance. So I chose to have one time during every day, when I would do some physical exercise. I did one of these three options: an exercise tape, a walk, or a swim in the local pool.

These times for my own well-being were important to me and I kept my appointment with myself daily, even when I had to ask a neighbor to sit with Mom when I was out, even when, during the later days, Mom didn't want me to leave her. Still, I did my exercises. I needed to do something that signified I was separate and that I was still healthy and alive. These brief times of respite when I was focusing on my own needs, were times of peace and renewal. I was in training for a marathon of caregiving and my time apart was crucial to stay the course. I'd return to Mom refreshed, energized and full and ready to put in the next twelve to sixteen hours that she needed.

Eventually, I did ask for help when the strain of it all felt like it would crush me. Certainly, asking for help is a healthy action. We really don't have to do it all by ourselves. I needed to give this care in the all-consuming way that I did, to stretch the limits of my strength and compassion, but I also needed to replenish my strength on a regular basis in order to do it.

You who are caregivers must realize that you need your own self-care. It's important to dedicate yourself to some physical, emotional, spiritual activities daily in order to survive in supporting your loved one. Caregiving can take all you can humanly give, and deplete you so much that you may want to say to your loved one, "Move over. I'll join you in the grave."

There are many other self-care practices that nurture and replenish. Meditation, prayer and body work, like massage and energy work, are just a few practices to consider in balancing your own being. Choose well what will support you physically, emotionally and spiritually. Establish a meaningful routine and do something daily as an expression of self-love to fuel the support and love you are giving.

## Asking for Help

When you become a caregiver, many friends and relatives will ask, "Is there anything I can do to help you?" Your response is often an automatic, "No, I'm fine," because you feel the person is just expressing a nicety and doesn't really want to do anything to help. You may not even know in what way you could use help. This is why, when we do offer assistance, it's best to be specific. For example, we could say, "I'm going to the store. What can I get for you?" I encourage you to really stop and think when you are given this open-handed expression of support and loving kindness and resist any reticence to request help. When you accept the love someone wants to give, everyone feels better and your loved one is cradled in a larger circle of care and concern.

My time with Mom trained me in asking for assistance. We were blessed with neighbors who heard our requests. Blessings like butterflies surrounded our home the day the

Brady family moved in next door to us. When I first met Hugh Brady, I experienced in him such a presence and depth of compassion and wisdom and integrity that I wished he could become the President of our land! I imagined what a difference such a consciousness could make in that high office. Hugh's wife, Evelyn, quickly became the emotional glue of our neighborhood. She and one of her sisters, Nurse Jan, are cut from the same cloth of loving through service and caring for others. They are consistently present for others with generous and open hearts. I still think of them as our angels of mercy.

Evelyn offered to take walks with me, and I recall our times in the autumn, walking and breathing deeply as I reconnected with her and witnessed my neighborhood's renovations anew since I had been away for many years. And there were later walks with Evelyn in snow covered Delaware Park watching skaters on the frozen lake. I also asked if Evelyn or Jan might take turns sitting with Mom for an hour when I went for my swim. They kindly did that, enjoying some time with Mom, and she with them.

In retrospect, I realize how important it was that when Mom stopped eating for the final two weeks of her life, Evelyn made a little extra of her family dinner and sent a portion to me. This was invaluable help and such loving kindness. I didn't need to leave Mom's side to cook, when she was unable to eat and could barely sip water, I didn't have to surround her with the aromas of my cooking as she lay in the room next to the kitchen.

Much later, I asked my brother in desperation to come from Maine and share the load with me in Mom's final days when I was fighting exhaustion. He agreed, left his busy work schedule and a young family and we took turns staying up with Mom at night so that she was never alone.

We also hired an additional home care aide who kept watch at Mom's side during the nights. You can ask for that extra help through Hospice or your health insurance coverage. Sometimes your doctor can requisition extra hours of home health care. Sometimes you will have to pay for it yourself, but it is money well spent.

One night I was ready to go for my swim and Jan came to stay with Mom. I knew I was leaving Mom in very good hands. That night, I suppose Mom was a bit frightened and she didn't want me to leave her. "Why do you have to go for a swim, anyway?" was her lament. I was momentarily stopped but Jan intervened and said that I had to do this. It was important for my well-being and there was nothing to worry about. I was grateful for the stand Jan took on this because I needed to swim! Being in the water I felt cleansed of the stress and sorrows of the day. I swam laps for an hour— rhythmical, long arms and legs, stretching and pulling, supported by the invisible buoyancy of that water. Breathing deeply and keeping time with my strokes allowed me to think things through and my tears dissolved away without a trace or a sound in that expansive pool. I'd end my time of silence with a sauna, re-igniting my inner warmth in this winter of despair.

Not everyone needs to make the choice I made, risking so much to be with my mother at that time. Not everyone wants to be with the person who is dying. Not everyone wants to be there at the moment of their death. It is a very individual decision and we all need to honor whatever choices are made.

Sometimes, a parent will seem to be waiting to die until the last child comes to be with them and the family. It really appears that once they see that child, they can let go and leave within a day. Sometimes it is not for us to be with that parent in their dying. By our absence, the other siblings get the opportunity to give of their love and share valuable time that would have been difficult or impossible to do if the other child had been present.

Caregiving around the dying process is as multifaceted as the interpersonal relationships in families. Honor each person's choice but, as a caregiver, ask for your needs to be met as well.

## Communicating with Others

I shared a wonderful resource in Chapter Two called, *A Keepsake Journal*. These books are designed to chronicle family history. I recorded Mom's comments as we conversed together about her life. Later, a friend typed up that audio tape for me. This is a simple way to encourage a detailed conversation of reminiscence so vital to a person. Communicating a life review is an important part of aging whether there is illness or not. I suggest that you try to do this retrospective before your loved one is too weak to really talk much.

So many people wanted to know how Mom was doing. This was before email and texting, so they would phone us. My usually gregarious Mother began to close in and didn't want to talk with others. While I appreciated our friends' concern, I found I was repeating the same details in call after call. It became disruptive to Mom's peace and tiring to me. I decided to write letters and made copies of them and sent them to our family and friends in the U.S., co-workers in Miami and relatives in Czechoslovakia. In these musings I could go into more detail about our days. People appreciated knowing and having a way to be a part of this process and we all enjoyed more connection with each other as our relatives and friends were kept in the loop. These days we could easily use email to accomplish the same thing. Also, there is a free web site, www.caringbridge.org, which anyone can use to chronicle and share the progress of their loved one facing a health crisis.

I invited our friends and family to join us in prayer at five p.m. each day and to send a photo of themselves, or a card that I placed on a tag board at the foot of Mom's bed so she could see all those who chose to be with us in prayer. During our nightly prayers we remembered each of those dear ones as they prayed for Mom. Of course, if five p.m. wasn't the best time, they were encouraged to pray at a time more convenient for them. Prayer is timeless. We set out to do this prayer practice for the whole month of November and we felt connected to and surrounded by their love.

After our daily prayer practice at five p.m. and supper, Mom and I would watch TV and share her favorite treat of ice cream and cookies. While she relaxed, I did Reiki (hands-on energy work) on her abdomen which helped to ease and soothe her pain. She always appreciated receiving that loving touch and was amazed at how warm my hands became from that flow of energy.

Following are excerpts from the first letter I wrote.

*Tuesday, October 18, 1988*

*To Our Dear Friends,*

*I know my mother and I are in your thoughts and prayers and that you are wondering how we are...*

*As it turns out, it is even more crucial for me to be here than we first thought. Right after I arrived, we discovered that my Mother's significant other, Bob, has advanced brain and bone cancer throughout his body. The doctor gives him only a couple of weeks to live . . .*

*None of us had any idea he was so sick and he never let on that he thought he might be. We are all devastated . . .*

*This is the first time in four years that I have seen a northern autumn. The days are bright and crisp and the leaves are in full color . . . Little remembrances return of this time of year, the angle of the light and early evening darkness and the smell of wet leaves and Halloween. My home is dearer to me now because I know that soon it will no longer be my home base. How strange to think that in the near future the place I called home for twenty-five years will be closed to me. I will never again be able to just open the door and walk in . . .*

*I showed the downstairs apartment to the new lower flat tenants today. Their excitement and appreciation of the house reminded me of what we felt when we found it: the elegant spacious rooms...the delicate leaded glass windows, the porches, the yard and the garden and of course, my favorite three lilac trees . . .*

*I am reminded of a scene in Anton Chekhov's play, <u>The Cherry Orchard</u> in which the main characters are selling and leaving the family estate. Like all of Chekhov's writing, there is a mixture of tears and laughter. In this scene the brother, sentimental about his life, recites a sincere farewell ode to a simple mundane bookcase! Of course, everyone cracks up laughing, but I think I know how he felt.*

*Mom and I have very full days because she needs a lot of care and cannot go out . . .*

*I find that I have been reflecting a lot about life and death and am reading a great book by Stephen Levine, titled, <u>Healing into Life and Death</u>. This is from the chapter, "What Is Healing?"*

"So it became evident that a preparation for dying, a new opening to life, allowed deeper healings to occur. For some, these healings affected the body as well as the heart. As Ondrea and I began to investigate what healing might be, the context rapidly expanded. If healing was as it seemed, the harmonizing of the disquieted, a balancing of energies to bring about *peace where before there had been none, then healing clearly was not limited to the body, or even the visible. It includes the possibility of quieting even the deepest unseen wounds—the discomforts which make death seem a respite.*

*"Indeed, in trying to define the work we do (healing and working with the dying), the difficulty of limiting healing to any particular level became more apparent. If healing is as it seems, the integration of body and mind into the heart, then our only direction has always been healing. Healing is the growth that each person seeks. Healing is what happens when we come to our edge, to the unexplored territory of mind and body, and take a single step beyond into the unknown, the space in which all growth occurs. Healing is discovery. It goes beyond life and death. Healing occurs not in the tiny thoughts of who we think we are and what we know, but in the vast indefinable spaciousness of being—of what we essentially are—not whom we imagined we shall become."*

*This passage inspired me and expanded my understanding of healing. I hope it is equally helpful to you, as well.*

*Love,*
*Patricia*

## Communicating with Self

Journaling your thoughts and feelings, especially, is a great way to express your deepest honesty. Journaling is a way to articulate in an uncensored way everything— even the pieces you would tend to hide from someone else. You can let it all hang out in your personal journal and no one else ever has to read it.

I kept a journal where I shared my thoughts about Mom and what I was feeling. My journal became a profound method of communication for me and a practice I could do after my daily chores were complete.

Because I didn't have much time to speak on the phone to others about my feelings and thoughts during my caregiving, my journaling became an important part of my self-care. It was an outlet for my raw feelings and deepest honesty where I came to express and eventually understand myself in a completely private setting. My journal became my most trusted confidant, crucial for my own emotional balance.

Journaling actually creates order where there has been or still is chaos. It helps us to make sense of the senseless. Journaling helps to end personal confusion because the communication is between various parts of yourself. To me, it feels like there is a lively dialogue, a dynamic conversation between my conscious self and my Higher Self, informing and guiding my conscious self, without any barriers, without any filters on my truth. In retrospect, the journal I kept during Mom's final months reveals and clarifies so much to me now. I share the following pages from my journal with you to encourage your own full expression. When you journal, hold nothing back. You can write about how very angry you are, for example, and express and eventually accept that part of you without harming anyone with your anger. Journaling is not just a rote record of what happened. It can become a sacred process. It became that for me.

# SACRED PROCESS

## EXAMINING OUR THOUGHTS

Unconscious, unexplored beliefs can control your life and limit your expansion. Beliefs can be a bit elusive. They may be tricky to uncover because we act from our beliefs. Yet we can uncover them. Seek to find clarity to know what you are believing. You will then have access to change your beliefs if they are not supporting the best life you wish to have.

Are you willing to identify your beliefs about:

1. Death—is it the end, or a beginning, or a pause in the continuation of eternal life, or something else?
2. In general, what do you say it means when someone dies? What does your loved one's death mean to you? (Now that my _____died, my life is_____.) Your own death?
3. Dying—do you believe you have to die in a certain way—through the same illness or same age or scenario as your parent? Does death and dying have to be hard?
4. Are death and pain punishment for your sins, or is death a natural part of life and a way your soul expands? Is death scary because of your belief, or lack of belief in the afterlife? Your beliefs about God?
5. Are you willing to cross out death as your enemy and know that you are not diminished by death and dying? Are you stronger than death? Do you believe love is stronger than death? What does "love is eternal" mean to you?
6. What do you think about the idea that everything lost is replaced by something greater?

7. What does finishing your emotional business look like in your life?
8. Have you tied up loose ends by writing a will, communicated your wishes for your medical directives, living will, and funeral wishes?
   (There is a pamphlet that can be helpful with these issues called "Five Wishes" found at www.agingwithdignity.org 1-888-594-7437.)

# CHAPTER 5

## My Journal

DESPITE MY EMPHASIS on Mom in the following journal pages, it's important to acknowledge the help she had from a loving friend. Unfortunately, he died before Mom did. That is why these first journal entries about Bob appear first.

## BOB

### Sunday, October 16, 1988

I have wanted to get back to writing this whole week now that I am in Buffalo again.

When I arrived, I discovered that Bob, Mom's significant other, hasn't been out of bed for a week. I'm glad I asked Mom's visiting Hospice nurse Marlene, to look in on Bob, since we all have come to completely trust her. She was alarmed by Bob's condition. I drove him to his doctor's office and Doctor G. had me take Bob to be admitted to the hospital immediately.

We have had a terrible shock. Dr. G. called to give the results of Bob's tests. He said the chest x-rays he took of Bob in May didn't show anything, but now Bob has a large tumor on his lungs which has spread to twelve various size tumors on the brain, the liver and the spine. The tumors on the spine answer the question of the pain in his back he's been mentioning. Bone cancer is said to be one of the most painful cancers that exists.

Bob had a grand mal seizure this afternoon and is in the intensive care unit. He hasn't come out of it. His doctor says that Bob is in no pain, his eyes are open, but he is not responding to what is being said. Doctor G. will advise Bob's family to agree not to resuscitate him, if he begins to fail. His doctor gives him about two weeks if he doesn't come out of the haze from the seizure.

I feel so sad. Bob kept going and caring for Mom until I came home this past week to take care of her full time. Then he collapsed. He is such a silent-suffering, isolated man, forever keeping his internal state shrouded in mystery. What was he feeling, what were his thoughts and fears about Mom's situation and his own? He kept it all deep within him.

I know that he loves Mom very much. He has a sense of duty and responsibility that is complete and extreme and even if he was suffering, as he must have been, riddled with cancer, he never complained about his pain. I suppose he didn't want to upset Mom in her condition.

But I wonder how could it be that Bob's x-rays taken five months ago wouldn't show any tumors before developing twelve of them? Perhaps these are rapid growing tumors. I wonder if his thoughts around Mom's dying and eventual death, might have caused him to choose death himself. Our thoughts, and especially, those unexpressed feelings can be so powerful that it's not unusual for one partner to follow the other one swiftly into death. I mourn not only for Bob's dying, but I mourn for the constrained life of this very good man who lived such a withdrawn existence removed from the human comfort that could have been his.

I look at his garden in our backyard which is a living representation of Bob. We always teased that "Farmer Bob" had two green thumbs. He could turn any landscape into bountiful production more completely than anyone else I've ever known. And now the tomatoes are lying there in the dirt, dying on the vine.

I feel a heavy sadness when I am in contact with the personal objects that are a part of Bob, the things he touched, like his garden, his car and other possessions. They weigh on me. They hold a nagging responsibility calling for me to do something with them, or save them as proof that the person existed. "Do not lose them," something cries, "for they are all you have left of that person." I dread that this burden will be even stronger when Mom dies. How will I ever throw things away that she has touched?

I think I should visit Bob tonight at the hospital and give him some hands-on healing energy. I wish I had opened my heart to him more. I have strong memories of how he defended me in a difficult situation and how he tried to bring some healing to that experience.

I recall after Mom's operation when he and I were stabilizing Mom as we walked at Front Park near the lake. I thanked him for being a great support to Mom, and he was shy in the face of the acknowledgement. I'm so grateful that Mom told me to tell him she loves him when I went to visit him Friday, just two days ago. That was the day before he became so confused.

Sometimes, when Mom wakes up, she calls to me, "Bob."

Everything is dying; my family, my connection with my home, my history in this beautiful house, even the abundant garden.

## Wednesday, October 26, 1988

Bob died at 2:15 p.m. today. John, his brother, called us about 2:30 p.m. to let us know.

Mom had been advised by Nurse Marlene, just minutes before the call from John, to take a full Xanax rather than half because she seemed anxious. It is a good day for her to have more tranquilizer.

I'm glad I saw Bob yesterday. I kept telling him to "go toward the light" and today to help myself I'm repeating, "He's free, at last." That's what Mom said when I told her that Bob died. She added, "His suffering is over."

I asked our aide, Chantelle, to pray with Mom and me. She said, "We mourn when we're born and rejoice when we die. We pray for Bob's journey back to our Father." Then we three prayed the Our Father and Mom asked that Bob's soul have eternal peace. I asked that each of us visualize Bob going to meet God, enfolded eternally in Divine comfort and peace.

Mom asked me if I was crying and she said, "I can't cry" which made me cry even more. I said. "I'll share my tears with you." I'm not sure why she couldn't cry. Perhaps it was the medications that she was on. What a loss not to be able to express one's tears when feeling such sadness.

As I write this, I am drawn to look outside, the place I most identify with Bob. It has been so dark these days. The sky is dark gray with heavy, low clouds. It's a wintry gray day that all Buffalonians know.

When I looked out the kitchen window, the sun peeked through and the sky began to clear. A big, white billowy cumulus cloud blew swiftly by on the wind. The sky was blue in minutes and in that improbable lightening of the sky and the re-emergence of light in my mind's eye, I imagined Bob being greeted by his brother and others, but also by my Dad. Of course, they would recognize each other although Bob only knew Dad through photos. Dad would greet Bob and warmly thank him for helping to take care of his family. Of course, my uncles Joe, John and Mike, are lined up like the three musketeers smiling at Bob. No doubt they are getting ready to sit down together to their customary game of cards.

It is said that when we die, we are greeted by family and friends as we make our way toward the eternal and magnificent light of the Divine. My fantasy of my father and Bob meeting in the afterlife, was my wish for a reconciliation, not only between those two souls, but also said something about what I needed.

In truth, I never let Bob completely into my heart. I always felt uncomfortable that Mom and he were seeing each other, even though Mom waited about four years after Dad's death before she started dating. Somehow, I felt like she was betraying Dad. Of course, this isn't logical, but it was difficult to accept anyone other than my Dad as my Mother's significant other. It seemed that because Bob was significant to her, he was supposed to be significant to me. I didn't know exactly what he was to me. He couldn't take the place of my father, and yet, there he was in a type of "head of the family" role. It was unsettling and I never talked about it.

Mom chose not to marry Bob. He had never been a parent and was somewhat rigid in his views about raising children and Mom didn't want him to try to interfere with the ways she and my father agreed to raise us. She felt it would cause conflict in the home and be confusing to my brother and me. And yet, they remained together for nineteen years and I knew Bob four years longer than I knew my own father; but time makes little difference in matters of the heart.

So my mother sacrificed remarriage for her commitment to us. I know that she made considerable concessions because our welfare was her priority.

Somehow, having another man as a father figure in our family finalized Dad's death to me in an odd way. I felt like, "Ok, we're done grieving? We're going to forget about Dad now? We're moving on? We're going to live again and be happy again?"

I also know now, that a time of discussion and processing those uncomfortable feelings together as a family would have made a world of difference to all of us. These wouldn't have been easy discussions, probably messy. If we had told our truths, perhaps we all could have let Bob into our hearts more. I wonder if Mom ever made peace with the fact that although Bob was a very good man, kind and generous, loyal and honest to a fault, yet he wasn't and never could be her first love and husband, Leonard.

## A Reflection

What does a spouse do after their loved one dies? How does one come to live again and love again?

I've seen a childless couple follow one after the other to the grave. She died and within a couple of months, he joined her. Family members said, he couldn't live without her that he died of a broken heart. I've seen widowers and widows find someone else to love who remarry and raise children together and balance a blended family. I've seen a bereaved spouse never engage in another romantic relationship and remain single, perhaps because they wished to find no one else to love. I've seen a few who pick up with a new love right after the death of the first, shocking the neighbors, and continue into a lasting relationship.

Do any of these scenarios define the depth of love the person had for their lost spouse? I used to think that love was finite and that if you really loved someone, you couldn't add anyone else; that your heart could be filled only with that one person. But I've come to see that love is expansive and the space of our heart is limitless in its ability to hold more than one person at the same time in our love.

Perhaps it's easier to understand this concept by observing how a parent can fully and eternally love more than one child at the same time and the love the parent feels is never diminished by loving all the children. The more we love, the more we can love.

*Thursday, October 27, 1988*
*Dear Bob,*

*I'm glad I was able to give you MariEl (a form of hands-on healing energy work) on Friday. I don't think you resisted it. I regret that I wasn't with you today when you died, but my wish that you not die alone was granted. I'm relieved that your brother John, and sister-in-law Grace, were there with you.*

*I was so pleased to be able to offer you and Mom a place to stay with me in my home in warm Miami for your last winter.*

*I will always be grateful for your help in standing up for me verbally, physically, and emotionally. You were such a great help, my protector, during that very difficult time in my life and I also know how hard it was for you to do what you did for Mom, not feeling very well yourself. Although I've known you for nineteen years, there was still some distance between us. I found you a bit difficult to get close to, but I love you and I have so much gratitude for all the acts of love and selfless service you gave to Mom and me and our family.*

*We will, of course, never forget you, and we all pray for your eternal peace; a peace and rest you most surely deserve.*

*With Love,*
*Patricia*

# Mom

As I journaled during this precious final time of my mother's life, I challenged myself to be a keen observer of her dying process and to honestly record my own responses. In rereading my journal, I noticed that my fear was prominent mostly because I didn't know what to expect. I share parts of my journal with you now in the hope that you will know the themes to watch for in your own or your loved one's process. My wish is to inform and prepare you for the dying process as much as I can, so that you will more easily live fully without fear in these difficult times.

## Monday, October 31, 1988
## "WATCHING THE CHANGES"

It has been a difficult few days for me and for Mom. She remarked how strange it is that she can't cry. It bothers me as well that she is unable to cry. I know she feels the sadness but she has a flat affect, either from the drugs or the cancer or both. I'm glad I can cry, even though it hurts when I do. I imagine it would be worse if I couldn't cry. All that pain stuck inside.

I've seen a change in Mom since Bob's death. On Wednesday she had to take two tranquilizers. On Thursday, she was so upset when family members came to get Bob's clothes and belongings. Chantelle, our caring aide, sat with Mom and soothed her with her gentle, soft singing. Thursday night was the worst I've seen her. She woke up four times and had great difficulty walking to the bathroom. I was very frightened that I wouldn't be able to move her, or that she'd die that night because she was so groggy and weak. Friday morning she couldn't eat her breakfast, so I helped her to lie down on the couch, and she slept with me next to her. I prayed the rosary and it really helped me to stay calm. I felt the power of prayer. I was supplanting fearful thoughts with prayerful words and ideas.

When Mom awoke on Friday, I told her I'd said the rosary. She seemed very pleased and smiled. She was a little better for the rest of the day. However, Joyce, her Hospice nurse, came and had to catheterize her. When I told her Doctor P. about this, he said perhaps she's getting near the end and she is dehydrating. He said that's not a bad thing and for me not to push too much fluids.

I felt I was being placed in a difficult position. It feels like I'm not supporting her living by not giving her liquids, so I figured a compromise. I put her glasses of water and juice next to her and asked if she wanted some. I do what she requests. She isn't drinking a lot.

Chip's visit seemed to settle her and me. She slept well Friday night and he got her up the first time. It was reassuring to have someone else in the house with me. He left Sunday at ten a.m.

## Tuesday, November 1, 1988
### "CONSERVING ENERGY"

Spent a good day today. I was occupied most of the time that Chantelle was here.

Went for a swim and then lunch and then raked the leaves—four lawn bags full. It feels great to be outside and working. I can feel that my muscles have been used. I spoke to a neighbor and he said two more of our neighbors have cancer. It seems that this block is full of cancer.

My friend Carm says the beginning of life is a lot like the end. My taking such full care of Mom is like a mother with a new born. She advised me to rest a lot in order to save my energy for the most important task of holding her hand.

Good point. Rest when I can. I can do outside things later. They will still be there.

As I write, Mom is in her chair. She looks so sad. I tried to let her know she is part of me and I will never lose her. I think she understood.

## Friday, November 4, 1988
## "PAIN AND PAIN MANAGEMENT"

I was very angry today that Chantelle was forty minutes late. I was able to calm down and simply request that she be on time.

What an inner struggle I had in order to speak up, what a debate. Yet I did it. I took care of myself. Somehow I have always found the strength and courage to do what is important and go beyond my limitations, especially when it is for the benefit of a loved one.

Father Jeunker, our parish priest, came to the house and gave us Holy Communion today and he said he would join us in prayer at five p.m. as well.

Mom looks very weak and in more pain. I guess Nurse Joyce's substitute, Mary, was a problem for Mom. Poor Mom, I feel so sad that she is suffering. Last night she seemed very frustrated and took more morphine than ever before (eight pills) and she also took a tranquilizer to sleep during the season premiere of "Dynasty." This is a bad sign. She always loved that program so much but just couldn't bear to stay awake to watch it.

## Wednesday, November 9, 1988
## "THE THIN THREAD"

Sometimes Mom looks so beautiful. Her skin seems to be radiant. She is always amazed when people say how good she looks. I told her it is her soul shining through. At these times I think she'll live forever. Then sometimes she looks so gray and frightened and frail that I start to fear that she won't last the night. The energy of life and death is such a strange thin thread.

I spoke to my friend Annie tonight. I said I've noticed that "the love gets you through the hard parts." Sometimes I sleep only two hours with Mom getting up and never sleeping through the night. I do get crabby, but then the love gets me through. I look at her and I'm renewed. I also told my friend Annie how amazed and touched Mom was that so many people have agreed to join with us at the five p.m. meditation time. I'm so glad that Mom is witnessing and receiving that loving support. I guess love is getting her through the hard parts, too.

## Friday, November 11, 1988
## "CONVERSATIONS ABOUT THE END"

Thank God for Marlene B., Mom's trusted nurse. She saw Mom's willingness and had been waiting for it. Mom reached out her hand to her. Marlene asked if she is afraid of dying. Mom said, "No, because I won't know it when it happens. Or will I?"

Then Marlene described the reports of people with near death experiences: seeing the white light, seeing the Creator, meeting loved ones who have gone before us, feeling a wonderful sense of peace. She said that when these people were resuscitated, they knew they had to come back to life again because they had more to accomplish on earth. They almost felt disappointed at having to come back because they experienced such peace there. They also mentioned going into a place that can't accurately be described in earthly terms, but some say it's like a library or some place of complete knowledge and there they learn all the answers to the questions we can never find the answers to on earth. Then Marlene told Mom, "And that is what I hope for you."

Marlene said it all so simply and matter-of-factly, and Mom was with her echoing certain phrases to let us know she was there.

My prayers to find a way to get this message across to Mom were answered. Sometimes she would just shut me out when I tried to talk to her about death and sometimes I would start to cry which would make her close down. But NOW she HEARD IT! I am so glad.

Marlene said that that's her personality type. She keeps everything inside. It's strange. My whole life I thought she expressed herself and I didn't, but I realized now that she vented her anger at times but had a harder time expressing other feelings fully or easily.

Thank you God for this blessed opportunity to serve and learn. I love my Mom so much.

## Saturday, November 12, 1988
## "MOMENTS OF HUMOR"

Today a humorous thing happened. I want to hold onto these moments. Mom was in the bathroom with Marlene and the Meals on Wheels delivery lady was in the kitchen with Chantelle. I spoke to the Meals on Wheels volunteer and she looked at me and said, "You look a lot better than the last time I saw you." I said, "Well, I probably wasn't dressed at the time."

She said, "No you were lying on the little couch."

Chantelle said, "No this is her daughter!"

I think the woman was a bit embarrassed, but we all got a good laugh out of it. In this woman's eyes, Mom just dropped thirty-three years. No wonder she looked better.

## Sunday, November 13, 1988
## "SADNESS"

Today Mom had difficulty walking throughout the day. On rising she looked in the bathroom mirror and said, "I can't see out of my right eye." There was a moment of fear and horror; then she recovered and said, "I'll just rinse it." She had a little bit of dry heaves again, the second time in a week. I said the dry heaves reminded me of our cruise when I would hold her to ease the fear.

Later in the day, when Chip called to say he'll come Tuesday through Friday the week of Thanksgiving, Mom said she doesn't know how she'll be in two weeks.

Yesterday Dr. P. came and is reducing more of her meds as she doesn't need so much. He said it's because she has such a strong heart that she's lasting. Mom said, "What's the use of it?" He said, "It served you well for all these years." Even he didn't think she was seventy-one years old; she looks ten years younger.

I see Mom getting weaker and I am so sad. I love her so much. I cry for my family. I love them all. I wish I'd already transferred our old family films onto video because I don't know if I'll be able to look at them when she's gone.

The nurses say she's depressed. I guess so but I feel blind to it.

I want to ask Chip to do her portrait like he did Uncle John's shortly before he died. He's such a good artist. I hope he will do it. It could be a way for him to connect with her, too.

## Monday, November 14, 1988
### "WHEN TIME IS RUNNING OUT"

A very noticeable change in Mom: she snapped at me at dinner. I was just telling her about wanting to give Steve and Bernadette, the new tenants downstairs, some flowers as welcome, and she said I was pushing her. She snapped at me to stop it!

She was also very controlling from nine p.m. on and asked me to rub her legs as they felt stiff. Her left leg was very tense and hard. I think she was very frightened, losing control and so was trying to control me. It must be very frightening to feel the illness taking over more of one's body. Also, Marlene couldn't find any stool today. Back to the oil/syrup.

It is so strange to imagine her really dying. It feels surreal.

I took a half hour and went for a vigorous walk today. It felt good to be in the brisk air. I thought of a great project. I'd like to take photos of the beautiful Victorian era Buffalo homes and make a poster of them.

I feel so antsy like I'm not getting anything accomplished and time is running out.

## Wednesday, November 16, 1988
## "THOUGHTS ON NUTRITION"

I was thinking about that old saying that was bandied about in our home for as long as I can remember, "You are what you eat." Balanced nutrition was valued in our home because our parents wanted us to receive good building blocks for strong bodies. My parents were not alone in believing three meals a day with meat, dairy, sugar, a smattering of overcooked frozen vegetables and canned fruit was the recipe for health. It was the food pyramid promoted by our government that most everyone followed.

That makes the location of my parents' cancers even more ironic. Dad's naso-pharynx cancer burned his throat with scarring radiation that restricted his ability to swallow food as the scar tissue continued to close off this passageway. And years later, Mom had ninety percent of her stomach surgically removed, drastically limiting what she could eat.

In the late 70s while studying singing technique, my teacher made a comment one day that confused me. He thought I should try eliminating all dairy from my diet, as he felt it was clogging my throat and affecting the production of my vocal sound. I dismissed his suggestion as a strange abnormality because I was so unaware of the connection between food and body function. Around the same time, I read, *Sugar Blues,* by William Dufty. He revealed that white sugar is an addictive drug and extremely harmful to the body. This was also news to me.

I mention all this here because when Mom had her appointment with the nutritionist after her surgery, I was particularly interested in how she would advise Mom. She gave Mom a list of foods with lots of focus on saturated fats. She told Mom to eat plenty of dairy, ice cream and yes—bacon. I was shocked and upset because the news reports recently disclosed that nitrates in bacon were carcinogenic.

Mom was upset by my reaction. She simply wanted to follow the protocol and go home. Still I wanted to know, for myself, the rationale of the dietician. She said the goal of this eating plan was to keep Mom from losing too much weight—that's all. So I learned from her response that they weren't expecting Mom to heal, and the food wasn't designed to support her recovery.

Here was another piece in my letting go, in accepting her situation. She seemed to also be accepting it, by not having the energy to fight it. Our body eventually gets too tired out and this can actually be a help to overcome our core impulse to live, to survive, to go on.

## Thursday, November 17, 1988
## "THE LEARNING CONTINUES"

I believe in angels who bring messages from the Divine. They come in all kinds of shapes and forms. Today I answered the doorbell and there was a short, gray-haired woman with a slight German accent who said she wanted to talk to my Mother. Now I am not in the habit of ushering strangers into our home, but somehow, she was different. Perhaps I was welcoming because we were used to the parade of Hospice and home health care people making their way upstairs and into our dining room which had been furnished with Mom's hospital bed and all her support equipment.

This woman, I don't even remember if I asked her name, looked at Mom and told me that she heard Mom had cancer and that was why she had come. She announced that Mom needed to eat a healing diet of macrobiotics; this would cure her. She herself was ready to do the cooking to nurture Mom back to health. She began to roll up her sleeves.

I thanked this rather odd, but clearly dedicated and positive woman and told her that Mom was too far along to try something so new. The woman looked at Mom and me, shifted her zeal into acceptance and left as swiftly as she arrived.

I'm not sure what all this meant, but it reinforced my growing awareness that food is an important factor in health.

## Monday, November 21, 1988
## "SIGNS OF DETERIORATION"

Difficult weekend. Mom seems to be more confused and goes off on tangents. Today she was convinced that she'd taken her shower before she did. She was talking in her sleep and baring her teeth on Saturday. She asked if the man who lives here went out, naming my father who was long gone. I wanted her to be clear. She was so confused Sunday that I was sad and frightened to see her mind affected. I called her doctor when I realized she hadn't urinated all day. He said her lack of urination and her shakiness may be related to one of the medications which we are in the process of eliminating.

Tonight she slept with such a sad, weary, drained, look on her face that I wanted to cry. When I tried to rouse her to have her snack, she couldn't remember what she wanted to eat and then she dozed off again. Finally, I just held her head and did some energy work on it. When I see the signs of deterioration, I get so scared and resist her death. But other times I know she's not very happy here with this life, and I ask God to take her.

I think I'm afraid that I won't be able to be of help to her at the end, or I'll mess it up or not know what to do or who to call, or I'll be all alone, scared and crying and not be there for her when she needs me the most. I get in such an internal state of panic, like I am right now, that I can't do anything. That's what happened on Saturday. I had so much to do, but I couldn't focus and so I just sat with Mom and held her stomach.

I so love our hugs and when she calls me her little girl. Today she said how beautiful I was as a little girl with my long sausage curls. She had fun curling and taking care of my hair.

I spoke to my boss at the agency. He gave me until December 19, to return to work and said to keep in touch with him. I was surprised that he set such a deadline as there is no way to hurry death. He thought by December 19, I will have been here long enough and need to return to my life. I am sure he was trying to help me, but he really has no idea of the importance of my mission. I must tell him this is my life right now. That taking care of my Mother is so important to me that I feel if I missed this chance to be of service to her, the loss of it could impede my future progress in life. As much as I enjoy my work, some things in life are just more important than a job.

## Saturday, November 26, 1988
## "NOTICEABLE WEAKNESS"

Just realized it is exactly a month since Bob's death.

It has been a very eventful week. Today Jan came to stay with Mom so I could walk at Delaware Park. It was over sixty degrees today, warm and beautiful. I felt so renewed to be outdoors. Jan will return tonight to help Mom get into bed.

I started the day very positively. Mom timed her wake ups exactly right in order to take her morphine at three a.m. and then nine a.m. She was able to lift herself into bed for which I was very much relieved. Evelyn came last night to help boost her into bed.

I spoke with Jan yesterday on the phone. Since she is a nurse, I asked her whether to keep Mom at home or have Mom admitted into the hospital. Would she have better care there? She suggested that since the hospitals are understaffed and no one could give the same loving care that I can, that we should try to keep her at home until the time when I couldn't manage anymore. This felt right and I was relieved by this decision.

So I got up and exercised and wrote some affirmations and all was ready when Jan came and gave Mom her second breakfast. I had told Mom about my desire to have Jan come in order to go out. She looked at me with a face that said, I don't want you to go and leave me, but she said, "Okay," when Jan came and she greeted her warmly.

When I returned, I gave Mom lunch. She seems out of it today. Her eyes are out of focus, glazed, distant. She didn't eat very much, and I could see she didn't have the strength or desire to eat more, so I said, you don't have to force yourself, and she stopped eating.

From three thirty p.m. through five p.m. I sat next to her as she slept very soundly and I read my book. I woke her for prayers at five p.m. and she said in a very light voice, "Do I have to?" I said, "No, I'll pray for both of us." and she looked for a while at the collage of friends and relatives in front of her.

During this prayer and meditation time I was so aware of her energy waning, that I thought she might die just then. I remembered the Stephen Levine book saying to go beyond your own pain, and be there for your loved one. It's her show, I really can't screw up, I'll know what to do, I thought, I'm just a supporting player. The advice from the book was to be in touch with the universal heart/love. And that happened a little. It was a beginning. I was prepared at that moment to let her go. Then she woke up, her eyes slightly more in focus and said, "It's time to get up. Time to eat."

I found my scribbled notes from last Saturday, November 19, 1988, written while I held her stomach with my right hand and tried to write key words with my left.

That day she was very shaky and had tried to crack her soft boiled egg and lost balance and almost fell. Luckily, I caught her, but both of us were shaken. I remember she tried immediately to carry on even though the runny egg was lying in the sink. She tried to pick it up. I told her to stop. That quality is so her. She has such a will to keep going no matter what. "Can't see out of one eye—(pause)—well, I'll just rinse it, and go on." Marlene says Mom is walking out of sheer will.

Mom was talking in her sleep. She was clammy, but her temperature was normal. Dr. P. said after she has cold sweats, her temperature will return to normal. I noticed she seemed to be holding her breath as she slept, like she is in pain. Marlene said to notice that sometimes her breath will stop and be uneven. I already noticed that and wish I'd written when it started. I know that unevenness began the day I did the Buddhist practice of vocalizing "ahhh" while mirroring her breath. This is a process of being more fully present with the person by synching your inhale and exhale with theirs.

She is having difficulty lifting the spoon to her mouth. When she walks, it's like her eyes are focused within. I can see in her that she is completely, actively involved in the biggest battle of her life, even when she seems to sleep.

She asks me about who we are expecting; the aides or nurse, etc. She wants to be aware of what's happening. She asked me if we have everything organized.

Chip came Tuesday and we had a good talk Wednesday night. I cried and he hugged me. On Thursday, we went to our cousin Connie's for Thanksgiving dinner. Friday, Chip drew a picture of Mom. The three of us just sat in the living room and I wished that scene could go on forever. Chip drawing and Mom resting and me holding it all in my heart. I played some music.

Chantelle had to give Mom a sponge bath on the couch as she was too weak to get in the tub or sit in the bathroom on the little chair.

She had dry heaves before Joyce, the Hospice nurse came. The heaves were pretty bad earlier in the week. Wednesday she had them three times in the morning. Then I gave her a Compazine suppository for nausea and she seemed more peaceful after that.

Joyce found a lump on her right rear hip. It could be the beginning of a bed sore or the tumor growing. We will probably order a hospital bed to make her more comfortable.

Chip's presence helped me a great deal. He seemed to be in communication with Mom more than he was the previous visit. He got up at night and helped me to get her back in bed Thursday night.

I swam on Friday, but wasn't able to relax and heard Mom calling me inside my head. So I swam fast.

Chip brought me a quote that he thought would be a support to me. It reminded him of me:

"But they that wait upon the Lord shall renew their strength.
They shall mount up with wings as eagles
They shall run and not be weary
They shall walk and not faint." Isaiah 40:31

I was deeply touched that he shared this with me and saw me.

## Sunday, November 27, 1988
## "WANTING TO QUIT"

Sometimes I get to the point where I don't want to give anymore. I was watching a TV movie and at 10:45 p.m. Jan came in just at the climax of the story. Mom said, "Shut it off." I never did find out what happened. I feel that I'm being petty but also resentful. It was just a matter of fifteen more minutes.

Mom had a bad day. She tried to eat lunch and dinner and ate very little and had dry heaves three times. We did another meditation and it was very beautiful. I felt there was an energy of healing between us.

She seems to resent me going for a swim or leaving her. I suppose it is because I'm her life line now and she is very dependent on me. However, I will have to continue to take care of myself. I suppose she and I share that fear of abandonment and a need for closeness with our loved ones.

I called Marlene about the high blood pressure reading that Jan discovered and she said not to be alarmed unless it goes over 100–110 on the lower number. The reading is elevated because her heart is working harder. Jan said most often people with long term illnesses die of pneumonia. The heart becomes inefficient as do the lungs. The kidneys may fail or lose strength. It's a systemic thing.

Her stomach is so big with the tumor. It is so strange and sad for such a Mother to be as if she is pregnant with her death, giving birth to her eternity.

## Monday, November 28, 1988
### "PERMISSION TO STOP EATING"

I am very sad. Today Marlene told Mom she doesn't have to force herself to eat, just drink a little liquid when she gets to the point that it's hard to eat. Mom said, "I think I'm at that point." So Marlene gave her permission not to force herself. Mom said, "So what will I do then?" Marlene tactfully said, "The eating won't counteract the dry heaves." Mom said, "Oh, I gottcha."

When Marlene told Chantelle not to force the food, I found Chantelle with tears in her eyes. I was so touched that I held her around the shoulder and we cried together. She said, "You know, Patti, I love her, too."

I spoke to Chip and my sister-in-law Barbara about all that's going on, and I could tell they were very sad. They were supportive of me. Barbara said this is probably the hardest job I will ever have. They invited me to come to Maine and mentioned that Ben is really walking now.

Mom ate only a very small amount all day, just a little cereal which I had to feed her with a spoon, then an egg and a bite of toast and tea and a quarter of a glass of milk shake. Not even a full glass of water.

Mom is still funny sometimes. This morning, in the midst of dry heaves and feeding her the cereal, she winked at Chantelle and got a big rise out of her. Today when I came home from paying the last mortgage payment on our house, I felt such gratitude for all that Mom and Dad had provided that I kissed Mom and said, "I love you." She said, "My daughter, a little bit mushy." When I gave her a gift of lilac soap which is her favorite scent she said, "Are you trying to tell me something?"

## Tuesday, November 29, 1988
## "MORE THERE THAN HERE"

Myrna, a friend from work, called this morning and woke me up which I didn't mind as they are delivering the hospital bed early today. Myrna described the process well, "Mom is more there than here." It is sometimes so hard to wake her. During meditation I see her coming back into her body with a jerk sometimes when I count up to bring us back at the end of our session.

For some reason I feel lighter today. I have no idea why. I got a haircut and feel prettier, maybe that really helped. I played a game with myself and imagined nameless strangers around me kept admiring my new haircut as I shopped. Also, Barbara and Chip really understand where I am and they acknowledged me for what I'm doing. Barbara said very few would do the same and that she admired me.

Mom seems more confused and afraid of the changes in herself. Jan came over after dinner to help get Mom into the hospital bed but Mom thought it wasn't yet dinner time and told Jan to come back after seven o'clock. Jan didn't want to force Mom, so she left and came back later. Mom said, "Let's eat dinner. Why doesn't Jan get here?" I'm pretty much able to still decipher Mom, but she is less and less clear.

I told Mom again that I love her. She said, "Everyone does, even Chantelle said so and kissed me!"

Dear Chantelle, you came to us as a stranger, placed with us by an agency that doesn't pay you well for a job that is a life-line for our precious mother. There's a gentle sweetness about you, a goodness in your caring. I sense in you a hard life, interferences that kept you from what you know to do. You eat to calm yourself. And yet, your ability to soothe Mom with your prayers and gentle song is your beautiful heart expressing itself. I don't think you expected to love this woman, but you do and in that loving you have become one of us. We are sisters, taking each other's hands, helping to guide each other through the dark.

*Monday, November 28, 1988*

*To Our Dear Friends,*

*As I sit here at the kitchen table, my eye is caught by slight movement outside the window. It's snowing. Our first snow looks like someone has shaken feathers from a pillow. The flakes are so light and big and float lazily down. The seasons are now complete.*

*It is almost the end of November. I want to thank all those who were able to participate in the five o'clock p.m. prayers all month. The letters and calls and thoughts you sent meant so much to both of us and sharing your feelings helped me to feel not so alone.*

*Mom and I certainly felt a sense of the energy coming our way. Our work together was a success. Mom was presented with tangible evidence of the care and love and concern from our friends that is all around her. I felt renewed and pulled out of sadness and depression especially each day at that time.*

*Your initial commitment to join with us for the month of November is coming to an end. I intend to continue each day, for as long as possible, and anyone else is welcome to join us. I will continue to remember all our friend's intentions, whether you formally commit to continuing this process or not.*

# Accepting Death, Embracing Life

*Today once again, life mirrored art as I filed the papers to discharge the mortgage on my father's and mother's house. I heard the echoes of Linda Loman in <u>Death of a Salesman</u>, Act 4, speaking to her dead husband, Willie, "I paid the last payment on the mortgage today dear. We're free and clear." Everyday life has become such a polarity of emotions.*

*There have been subtle and profound changes in my relationship with Mom in the past week or two. Much of the time our communication occurs without words. Two weeks ago I saw incredible pain in her face all the time, even when she was asleep. Lately she seems much more comfortable for larger blocks of time, and she requires even less pain medication. There is a sweetness about her, never complaining or losing her temper—so easy to be with. Often her characteristic directness will come out of nowhere and her humor will lighten the day. Her eyes have somehow become larger and deeper blue. Sometimes they are clouded, but at times they seem to look right into my heart. People continually remark how good she looks! This constantly amazes her and she says she wishes she felt that good. But I think it's her luminous soul shining through. Her skin and face seem lit from within. She is now continuously in a hospital bed we placed in my favorite and most beautiful room that faces east. I call it the "dayroom," with its leaded glass windows and Damask rose wallpaper.*

*Modern medical science has given us the opportunity to investigate the dying process for a longer time. Levine says it's important to continue to live until the "right death." This is not an intellectual exercise, nor one that can be decided outside the individual, but an actual "battle" taking place. The whole life force to survive is in conflict with the letting go of death. An awesome process.*

*I am witness to an incredible battle here. My mother's will has always been strong and this time is no different. I watch her walk when anyone else would not be able to walk. The look in her eyes is one of sheer determination like you might see on a long distance runner just willing herself to reach the finish line, bleary eyed, but still moving.*

*If you believe that life is given in order to learn lessons, then the opportunity to learn must be ongoing and every moment precious all the way to the end.*

*Thanksgiving just passed and I have a great deal to be thankful for, especially for this opportunity to serve and love and learn so much. There are so many lessons. Certainly I'd have no problem being a nurse after this! I always asked for the chance to be conscious and aware during the dying process. I am learning to let go of fear of death, but during the times I fall short, through Mom's example, I am learning to live fully under whatever circumstances.*

*It's wonderful to see the love people have for Mom, especially our "support staff": her nurse's aide, Chantelle, and her special nurse, Marlene, and our neighbors Evelyn and Hugh and Evelyn's sister, Nurse Janice who are angels of mercy and help us in any way they can think of, and her Doctor P. who makes house calls to Mom and is available to her at any time.*

*I am grateful to all of you, my friends who enrich my life. I am also grateful that I have my family, my brother Chip, sister-in-law Barbara and nephew Benjamin who love and support me.*

*Lovingly,*
*Patricia*

# SACRED PROCESS

⟨⟩

## ANSWERING THE QUESTION WHY

The book, *As Someone Dies*, suggests that one write an answer to the question, "Why are you dying?" How would you answer this question for yourself or for a loved one?

I answered it from the perspective of why I think Mom is dying.

Perhaps to be able to do more effective work from the other side.

To separate from me—so that I will be on my own.

To teach me how to transcend death.

It's time—her work here is finished—although it's hard to imagine it. I feel that there is so much more she could do and accomplish.

I think she seemed to lose interest in life after her brain tumor operation fourteen years ago, and after Mark's death seven years ago, or was it after my wedding four years ago? Were these all little deaths to her and to her role as mother?

Could she be dying in order to give energy to her grandson, Ben from the other side? He is walking now.

Perhaps one must decrease so that the other increases.

⟨⟩

# CHAPTER 6

## The Heavens Open

As a person moves close to death, there emerges a palpable energy in their room, in the person and in those around the person. It is the thinning of the veil between the earthly reality and the reality of the spirit realm.

> For now we see in a mirror, dimly, but then we
> will see face to face.
> Now I know only in part; then I will know fully,
> even as I have been fully known.
>
> — 1 Corinthians 13:12

Accompanying the increased spiritual energy flooding this occasion, there is increased healing, creativity, ability, and beauty. It's as if the door to the other world is beginning to open to receive your loved one and the divine energy and light begins just to peek through the opening to help the dying person to transform from the solid human form and to separate soul from body. Those who are close can also feel the power of the rays of divine light flowing in through that opening door!

### Thursday, December 1, 1988
### "SPECIAL WORDS COMMUNICATED"

Yesterday was a good day for Mom, better than the last three or four days. Marlene speculated she was not over-taxing herself because now she is completely in the hospital bed all the time and uses the bedpan. Chantelle gave her a sponge bath with the new lilac soap and Mom liked it.

Marlene said the lungs filling up with fluid would probably only happen the last couple of hours, because Mom's lungs are very clear. She doesn't see a need to move her to the hospital unless a medical emergency occurs, so I guess she's home to stay.

Marlene suggested I use these good times to communicate anything to her that has been left unsaid, or to get Mom to talk because during the other times, communication will be impossible. In a way I feel everything is pretty much said, but the idea of the finality of this opportunity fills me with a heavy responsibility. Evelyn said I can't plan it. It must come from the heart.

We prayed at five p.m. and I think Mom was relieved to have our November commitment finished. At the end of our prayers she said "…and reward my ever-faithful daughter. That's most important."

Her prayer was so simply and eloquently spoken. It touched me very much.

It's snowing again.

## Friday, December 2, 1988
## "END OF LIFE HALLUCINATIONS"

Yesterday was a pretty good day. Mom was more present. I read to her the beautiful notes sent from Evelyn and from our friend, Jay. I cried and she comforted me and said gently, "No need to cry now."

I said, "I like it when you mother me and I also like taking care of you."

She said, "I miss you so much when you're gone during the day. I can't wait for you to get back. No one else takes care of me like you do."

I said, "I'll try not to be gone so long, but I do need to go out." I'm not sure she agreed.

She was happy to see Jan today. I spoke to Jan in private on the stairs and she believes I should continue to go out daily for blocks of time and that Mom is very fortunate to have me as most elderly are in homes where the staff is down the hall dealing with the more verbal or emergency patients.

This morning Mom went back to being more removed, less conscious, although not quite as bad as on Monday and Tuesday. She asked, "Where's Chip?" as I was struggling to reposition her on the bed. Her speech seems a little slurred and her thoughts are a bit confused.

## Friday, December 2, 1988 (Evening)

Mom is having end of life hallucinations. She woke up this morning and said in her take-charge-this-is-urgent-and-important-voice, "I have to get up and take care of the baby. Listen. Tell the girl back there to start with the baby. Everything is all laid out."

I said, "Okay, I'll tell her." Then tonight, just after I watched a 20/20 TV segment about a French woman scientist secluded in a cave for four months, I said, "Isn't that an interesting story, Mom?"

She said, "I think the other one was very interesting about the couple who are pregnant with the baby and they had to go into seclusion for nine months. It was the Graziano boy."

I asked, "Rocky Graziano?"

"No," she said, "The kid." Then I think she felt a little foolish perhaps and said, "Do you mind if I don't tell you the whole story?"

I said, "OK, but is the baby alright?"

She said, "It isn't born yet."

I wonder about this metaphor, especially since she is swollen with a growing tumor in her ovary. Nine months. December is nine months since March when we knew she was sick. It came to me that she has been in seclusion for these nine months and is in the process of giving birth to her new eternal life.

All these birth and death references keep coming up. Last night Jan said death is like birth because you never know when it will happen.

## Saturday, December 3, 1988
### "HER ONLY GRANDCHILD"

Mom seemed to look more drawn and tired and out of it today. She's talking more strangely again.

She asked me to come to her and move a glass on the shelf. I put my hand near hers and asked her to show me which way. She guided my hand a little to the left and then said, "That's good," and fell back asleep.

Then later when Jan came so that I could go for a walk with Evelyn, Mom said, "Patti, give the folks some food." I think she meant for Jan but I felt like she thought more were here. Maybe they are. Perhaps she sees many spirits hanging out.

Chip and Barbara sent a video tape of Ben crawling and walking! It was so great to see it. I cried for joy! Mom watched it very closely and said, "He's terrific! Glad to be able to see how far he's come and how much he's improved!"

I'm feeling so sad for Chip. He told Evelyn that Mom doesn't want to see Ben. This is unbelievable to me. Somewhere there's been some bad miscommunication between them. All I can say is death is not always tidy even when you have a lot of time to make it that way. I wonder if there's anything else I can do the help facilitate their reconciliation?

I just had a good talk with Jan after putting Mom to bed. I realized I needed to be the care giver to Mom, to experience this role reversal, in order to claim some of my personal power. I know that in growing up with my Mom, because she was so powerful, at times there seemed to be no room for me.

Now I am the mother. Jan said that there's no separation between us in Mom's mind. That's why she can't understand why I have to go out. If I just stayed with her everything would be fine. It's like when a baby is in its early stages, the baby is symbiotic with the mother. Their mother is their whole world. Jan said she feels I'm doing a great job and especially because I'm taking care of myself. Yes, I have made a real commitment to it.

I realized I will never be the same after this experience. I even look different; older and dried out. Oh, now, come on. It's probably just dry skin! But right now all that doesn't matter. I feel powerful and grateful for the chance to serve and to do it with love and without resentment. Thank you God.

See you again at five a.m. when my next shift starts.

## Sunday, December 4, 1988
## "THE FIRST DAY OF NOT EATING"

Mom said she's not feeling very well today. She seems groggier and it's difficult for her to articulate clearly, although I can understand her. She is still aware. Today she isn't asking as much for liquids and said that she didn't want her egg yet, maybe later.

It's a spectacular day, so, so bright. There is so much light inside the house and outside. Blue sky and gleaming, like how the light shines in Greece. I feel so cold—keep drinking tea. I'm scared—she looks so peaceful and is sleeping so much.

I made the call earlier to the Rubino Funeral Home to make the arrangements. I felt relieved.

I called Dr. P. and Marlene at three p.m. I realized she isn't asking to eat.

The rest of the day was a whirlwind. Marlene called and spent a lot of time talking with me, describing fluid retention, heart slowing down, etc. Mom may become incontinent so Marlene suggested getting Depends just in case because Mom is so fastidious. She said not to offer food because then Mom would feel like she should be eating. Just follow Mom's lead. Marlene said, "At some point, when you feel right, give her permission to go." Marlene gave me other helpful advice. She said, "Acknowledge her and appreciate all she did. Give her permission by saying things like; you put up a beautiful fight, you can be comfortable in letting go, hold her hand and say I have this hand and God has the other one, when you see the Light go toward it. I can share that I am ready too because of all the things you've given me. I am a strong person and have my friends and my work, and I am going to be fine because you've been such a model for me."

I had a good talk with Chip. I let him know how much I appreciated that he heard my need to have him with me when he came to be with us at Thanksgiving and I thanked him for being so supportive and present and helpful with Mom. I said that now I didn't feel I personally needed him to be with us at the end, but if that changes, I would try to be honest and tell him. But I really felt it would be better for him to experience this death with Mom. I told him this as a result of my understanding of life. I've found that if a person is willing to go into a difficult emotional place then they will have the chance of coming out of it better for having experienced it.

I also shared with Chip how terrible I felt because I wasn't with Dad when he died and that I missed being there by only an hour when I didn't relieve Mom at the hospital that morning. I thought that Chip has forgotten Dad because Dad died when Chip was ten years old. I reminded him that neither of us knew that Dad was dying. Chip remarked that he'd felt like Dad was mine and Mom's and that he'd felt left out. I don't want him to feel that way about Mom's death. I know it is his choice, but I definitely have my bias that he be here.

Chip said he felt that because Mom's illness was so long, that he resolved everything and said what he had to say. He asked me if Mom was still talking. I said she was, but it's not about talking anymore. It's about being with her and experiencing something.

He felt he could deal with it as well by being here or not. Then the analogy came to me to share. I know that the hospitals didn't used to let fathers witness the births of their own children. So if that were still true, Benjamin would still have been born whether Chip was there or not, but because of that experience Chip will never be the same. The birth of his son was a unique experience he witnessed and was part of. It could be the same with the death of our mother. I suggested he think about it and do what's right for him, not what's right for Barbara, Ben, me or even Mom.

Later Barbara called and spoke to Evelyn asking if she knows any babysitters for Ben. I'm so glad they decided to come.

## Monday, December 5, 1988
## "PERMISSION AND REASSURANCE"

What an amazing day. This is the second day that Mom hasn't eaten. Today we stopped all morphine and Halcion. She is only on Compazine for nausea, and is experiencing no pain.

Tonight there is more swelling in her feet and they are a little cold but when Hugh and Jan came over she was very alert. All day I sat by her and I felt good to do so. I just read some of the books on the dying process and it helped to prepare me.

Her breathing is so shallow, it is sometimes frightening to watch.

Marlene helped to get the ball rolling. She and I spoke it together, acknowledging Mom and giving her permission to let go and said we were ready too and that I would be okay. I also told her about going toward the Light and that as I held one hand she could imagine giving her other hand to the care of God.

Marlene felt she was really listening and Mom looked at me at one point with her clear eyes and said, "My daughter," very lovingly and proudly. I was so filled with emotion but I was able to pretty much contain it. Then her eyes started to roll back a little with half-closed lids.

Later she called me and said, "Help me. You've got to help me. I'm very sick." And later she said, "I don't know what I should be doing." I tried to reassure her that I will be here and that she's done everything she's supposed to do just beautifully and now she can relax and let go.

I told her, "I will help you in any way that I can. There are many souls helping you. Are you aware of them?"

"Yes," she said.

I wondered if she had forgotten our talk with Marlene. I know she heard it all when we spoke.

Tonight I am sleeping in the same room. We moved the couch next to Mom's bed. Evelyn will sleep here in case I need her. Jan said that if Mom dies at night, to call her and she will come over. What an amazing blessing to have such generous and loving neighbors.

Evelyn said that Jan told her that of all the patients she's seen, she's never seen anyone with more dignity than Mom.

## Wednesday, December 7, 1988
## "SPECIAL GIFTS"

I was awake most of the night Monday. Apparently Mom was not supposed to be completely off all morphine, so Monday night she was restless. Jan said perhaps she was in a bit of withdrawal. I was exhausted all day and chilled. I slept while Chantelle was here and did only half of my exercise tape.

Mom called for me while I was sleeping and asked for something to eat. I gave her a few bites of custard, made by her old friend Elisabet and that seemed to satisfy her.

I got up today and made sure I fed myself first because yesterday I forgot to eat until four p.m. Also, I was waiting for Chantelle to come to help me, but as usual, she was late. Her excuse was that she tried to get Mom's suppositories but the building was out of electricity. Oh, well. I feel she is frightened of being with Mom. I think she is fearing her death. I know that feeling well.

So I finished breakfast, exercise, showered and fixed my hair before anyone came. It felt so good to take care of myself.

Today Marlene and then Dr. P. came to see Mom. Mom has been sleeping a lot and was not able to really wake up when her favorite nurse and doctor came. Dr. P. sat with her for a while and I gave him a copy of my third letter. He read it and asked to keep it. He smiled at the mention of himself in the letter.

Today as I watched Mom, now completely confined to bed, her gaze on the wall paper in front of her, I thought she needs a beautiful picture that she can see from her bed and enjoy. I decided to look for one in the prints that Pier 1 sells, but I knew I shouldn't be away from her very long without coverage.

So I had a clear intention to find the right and perfect print as I set out to the store across the street and down the block. I hoped to find one with moonlight shining on the water. The idea of this scene seemed so right for Mom. She loved the moon and she loved the beach. Each time Mom and I did a visualization of a place of peace and serenity, Mom would go to a different beach. The last one was Crystal Beach in Canada where our family spent many happy summers. Another time she mentioned the foot of Michigan Street where she'd played as a girl and at other times she mentioned other beaches as well.

At that time, I wasn't so aware of how a clear intention can manifest your heart's desire, so when the first print in the rack was perfect, I didn't believe my eyes. I continued to search through the stack and when I came back to the first one, I realized what Spirit had given to me so quickly and easily.

The print was titled "A Little Girl on Skagen Beach at Sunset." It was a painting of a young girl and it was clearly set in an earlier time. (Later I discovered the artist was Peter Severin Kroyer, 1851–1909, who became the most famous of the Danish "painters of light" of the nineteenth century.) The girl is standing on the shore of a lake and there was a round heavenly body in the sky casting its beams on the water. In my excitement I imagined that girl in the picture as a young Anna Marie in a white dress with a sailor-ish hat standing on her beloved beach next to the lake. I was a bit disappointed thinking that it was the sun in the picture; the moon would be better. I didn't realize until I rushed back to Mom and hung the picture on the wall that I was seeing was not the sun, it *was* the moon, Anna Marie's beloved full moon! No matter how many times she saw that shining ball in the sky, she would exclaim, as if seeing it for the very first time, "Oh, look at that beautiful full moon."

There it was, just as I had asked for, casting its radiant moonbeams on the lake and on us as well. Oh, for Mom to be able to see that beloved full moon one more time. My inner voice in the store kept saying, "Why are you continuing to look. This is the perfect print!" Finally I stopped and bought it. I will take that picture with me when I leave here and it will always remind me of Mom. Mom loved the picture and thanked me.

As I sat next to Mom and she began groaning. I asked her what's wrong. She said, "I'm dreaming again, getting dressed to go out, but it's hard to get dressed here."

I said, "Just let me know if I can help you in any way."

Later she said she had to pick up a jacket from our neighbor Joe that she will need when she goes out. I told her I'd pick it up for her.

Chip, Barbara and Benjamin came to see Mom at seven-thirty p.m. She beamed at Ben and said several times, "He really is a lovely boy." She tried to hold his hand but seemed a little weak. She talked to him and called him and asked about his walking. Barbara said that he walks better every day.

When they were leaving, Mom tried in her gracious way to provide for them asking if they had enough of what they need.

Then about eight-forty p.m. she started very labored breathing. It was as if she was holding her breath and then trying to release it. Her eyes rolled up with half closed lids. I felt very stuck, like I couldn't leave her. I couldn't call Jan or Chip or anyone, so I just tried to be there.

I asked her if she could see the light—"Yes."

I asked if she could see God—"Yes." So I told her to just relax and go towards the light and that she is safe.

Then after twenty minutes she seemed to rouse herself and said, "Where are my brown pants, the ones I had on before Chip came? Get them because they're coming to pick them up."

I finally called Jan but she was at work. I called Marlene. She said her pulse had been 120 today, as it is now and her breathing was stopping like now. But I counted only about five breaths per minute.

Later Mom asked me if I was worried. She kept asking me, "What else?" until I said, "I was worried that you were dying just then."

She responded "Oh, well don't worry."

I asked her if she is worried. "No, because there is nothing anyone can do about it."

"Does it worry you when I am worried?"

"Yes."

"Okay, I won't worry anymore. I just hope I can be with you when the time comes."

Marlene suggested I call Chip to stay with me until Jan comes.

## Thursday, December 8, 1988
## "LABORED BREATHING"

Mom has had labored breathing for fourteen hours starting from last night around eight-thirty p.m. She asked me to help her at nine-thirty a.m. and call the doctor to let him know she's having trouble breathing.

Lisa, the new aide, was here last night to cover for me and yet I had such a difficult night. I had a headache from neck and back tension that remained all night long.

Last night while in bed I had a strange experience. I'm not sure if it was a vision or a dream. I felt like I was Mom. I was in her hospital bed and I saw her sheets and pillows around me and I was dying. I was breathing her breaths. It was so frightening.

## Friday, December 9, 1988 (12:30 a.m.)
## "SAYING GOODBYE"

Chip is here and we are getting ready to go to our rooms for bed.

Mom is snoring good and strong like old times. It sounds so reassuring.

She has been laboring all evening and I could no longer watch the TV. She seemed not to want to take her pill for sleep. She said, "Why am I pushing it?" Later she apologized to me.

She said goodbye to each of us. "Goodnight Jan, and my daughter, and my son."

Jan said she saw a change in her from even last night. She had a fixed stare. Her eyes tend to drift and her right eye was a little blood shot. She had the lousy dry heaves again as we were getting her ready for bed.

I am afraid not to be with her.

## Friday, December 9, 1988 (11:30 p.m.)
### "BEGINNING TO LET GO"

I am back on my shift with Mom. As Jan and I were getting Mom ready for bed, she said, "What's going on? I want to get this straight. I thought we were visiting."

I said, "I know, some nights it's hard to go to bed."

All day, she kept getting close to the end and her pulse would drop. She looks like she's shrinking. She's so tiny and her face is so thin. We had a five p.m. prayer time tonight and it seemed like old times, just the two of us in prayer. I love our quiet times together at night.

By five-thirty p.m. I heard some rasp in her breath. Marlene came twice today. She said that rasp is upper bronchial, not in the lungs. I think she almost left us at six p.m., but then everyone came back—Hugh, Marlene, Chip and she did too. No wonder people usually die in the early morning when everyone is asleep. The rest of the time can be so noisy and busy and I can see how it can pull you back to life.

I'm realizing how important it is that I be unafraid so she can go with me near her, not with a lot of others, quietly and easily and peacefully. So when I laid down in bed last evening, I tried to let go of the results. If she dies with me present, fine; if not, fine. And during our prayer time I realized I wasn't afraid. I felt I was one with the universal love, not only the personal love. So, I hope, I am ready.

This morning when I got up, I had a joyous feeling like the expectation I might have knowing she is going on a wonderful trip. Last night our schedule worked so well that half of the night I stayed up and then Chip relieved me for the second half. I feel rested and renewed.

I love her so. She called me, "Dollie" today and said she loves me.

Now I just want to be here for her and hope she can go on her journey peacefully, whenever she is ready.

Mom wanted to give Chantelle her Chanel #5 perfume as a little gift. Mom was so weak she couldn't talk to Ben today on the phone.

## Sunday, December 11, 1988 (12:45 p.m.)
### "THE STRUGGLE CONTINUES"

I sit here with her. She is so drawn. She really looks like Jesus in his suffering. There is a part of me that can almost go into denial and believe she will never die and I can be happy accepting that and happy sitting here with her for the rest of my life.

Marlene just called and said she thinks what's happening with Mom is like what I described in my letter. It's an incredible struggle. Everything in her has accepted death but there is a part of her that is so strongly the life force that it keeps her here.

Mom is still alert and present. A large part of me doesn't want to leave her side because I want to see how it all resolves.

How will her particular death be for her, this remarkable person?

Evelyn said death is like giving birth. Sometimes we're overdue.

## Monday, December 12, 1988 (8:00 p.m.)
## "THE TRANSFER"

I want to get this amazing experience down on paper.

I was here this evening sitting with Marlene, waiting to hear from Critical Care on how to increase Mom's morphine drip flow.

I was thinking about what I would have for dinner. Evelyn has been so kind and generous in sending me a portion of the dinner she prepares for her family for over a week now and all I had left from Evelyn was two pork chops.

I am not very adept in the area of cooking. I don't really know how to put food together and come up with an entrée. Well, all of a sudden the idea came to me. What about scalloped potatoes with the pork chops on top? I started thinking about how much I would love to have some of Mom's scalloped potatoes. I realized I never asked Mom for her recipe and I didn't know how she made it.

I began to remember the main ingredient. Perhaps we have that essential evaporated milk in the cupboard. Mom always had a fully stocked kitchen but lately there hadn't been much stocking up. But way in the back of the cupboard I found one lonely can of evaporated milk. I found the other ingredients and I seemed to intuitively know what to do. The casserole came out so crusty golden brown on top, just the way Mom would make it. It tasted so good, really wholesome good, like the taste of Evelyn's food. I was so pleased that it worked, that I created something that was good and satisfying.

Perhaps my discovery of how to make the scalloped potatoes may not seem that miraculous. I suppose a case could be made that once you've had a dish, you could figure out how to make it. But for me, there was no figuring it out. I knew what to do. I had surety and clarity. I had the emerging thought that I had been guided to make this dish somehow by Mom. She had communicated with me. I saw in my mind's eye clearly how she had made this dish.

I am aware of information coming to me from my Higher Self, especially at times in my work with clients where wisdom I didn't know I had would appear. But this time felt different. Mom was now a piece and part of the voice within me. This was very new. Cooking was a perfect medium to wake me up to this ability, since I lack so much knowledge of how to cook.

I felt such joy as it became clear to me that she is in my heart and in my soul and she can reach me. So much of my fear of losing her has also been losing her wide expanse of knowledge and my access to it. It was coming clearer to me that her body is really only one part of the person I love.

I told Mom that I know now that she communicated with me beyond words; that our hearts are joined and she is in my heart. Death cannot separate us. I will never lose that connection and I see the possibility of transcending her physical death. It has been my greatest desire to learn not to be so personally devastated by death, and here before me was a way to begin that process.

I don't know if Mom completely understood or heard me, but I'm sure she knows in her inner awareness.

## Monday, December 13, 1988 (11:25 p.m.)
## "DRAWING THE LIONESS"

Mom is in rhythmical breathing. She has looked like a lioness for the past few days (?) or hours (?), with her mouth wide open, like in a roaring position. She has such a strong heart. Dr. P. said he doesn't think she's in pain. This vocalization pattern is the body's response to the dying process. I drew a picture of her in this state.

## Tuesday, December 13, 1988 (10:15a.m.)
## "BEING WITH HER BREATH"

Yesterday when we put Mom on the morphine drip she slept well until five p.m. when Marlene came back to increase the flow from 5–7.5 because Mom told Chantelle she was in pain. Marlene was here until about seven p.m. and Mom slept well until eleven p.m. when we woke her to turn her for the night.

Then we proceeded on a three and one half hour back and forth, calling Marlene to increase the morphine three or four times, each time waiting to see how it worked. Mom's and my frustration and panic were increasing.

Finally, at three p.m. it seemed like she was choking to death, so Marlene called Dr. P. to ask if we should increase the morphine. He asked me to give her a Compazine suppository and cut the morphine back to level ten set twenty-four hours ago.

She had some sort of a seizure as Chip and I attempted to put her on her back and yelled out, "Not on my side," or something and then had a convulsion after which she was limp like a dish rag. I was horrified. What had we done to her? I felt we were in way over our heads and I wasn't comfortable with the coaching I was getting by telephone. Where was the Hospice assistance? I wasn't a nurse and we needed someone more experienced to be with us.

I called Dr. P. for help at this point. He said it was more a muscle seizure than an epileptic seizure. I called Jan and she came as soon as she could. Marlene was going to come but she was an hour away and I thought at that point we were all right. So Chip took over and I tried to sleep. I was up a couple of times when Dr. P. called. We tried to increase the morphine to eighteen cc. but it only depressed her breathing as we watched for forty-five minutes. Dr. P. said to decrease it back to ten cc. again.

I got up at nine-thirty a.m. too afraid to be away from her.

She is rhythmically groaning and saying "uh-ah-ha" with each breath. Chip said she had another seizure at nine-twenty a.m. I only saw her catching her breath after the seizure.

I feel so weary. I don't know how she can keep this up. I keep repeating inside, "Let go. Your work here is done. What's left for you to do is to merge with the light. Trust the light, go toward the light. This form in front of me is only a small part of my mother who I love."

Marlene is having difficulty tracking down Dr. P. to requisition more morphine and this batch runs out in three hours.

I went on my shift at four-thirty p.m. and at four-fifty p.m. she had another seizure. This time it wasn't as frightening to me. Three a.m., nine a.m., two p.m., and now five p.m.—seizures.

She is calm and breathing very shallow. I can't find her pulse but that could be my lack of ability.

She has one little tear that comes out of the corner of her right eye every so often. It is so very sad to see it trickle out especially because she hadn't been able to cry these past months.

She seems very weak and her hands are a little cold. She isn't struggling as much.

I don't know what to do.

Just be with her.

Her breath stops and for some reason I feel like I am abandoning her.

## Wednesday, December 14, 1988 (4:45p.m.)
### "MOTHER OF MINE"

Today, although I have never written a song before in my life, I wrote a song for Mom in waltz time as I listened to her audible rhythmical breathing, (death rattle), and I sang it to her over and over through the day.

Mother of mine, I have a song to sing to you, all day long so you'll never be alone or afraid.

Each day of this time, I pray for you to be at peace and at rest.
Soon you'll see our Lord in heaven.

Mother of mine, I have a song to sing to you, all day long. You are in my heart forever more.

Mother of mine.

I have been so weary today. I slept very well last night, without a worry since Judy G. RN was here, but I don't feel rested.

I woke up listening to a conversation between Marlene and Judy. Judy said she felt she wouldn't be here all night because of the way Mom looked. They don't understand how she could still be holding on.

Jan called and I said, I really think something special is happening here. It's just too unusual that she hasn't taken any food and minimal water since Dec. 3—eleven days ago.

As I sit here, I remember that strange awareness I had a few days ago that I was my Mother in her death bed. That was Wednesday night, the first night that Chip was here. Perhaps she is waiting in order to have me know that she is with me and will be with me, or perhaps there is something else I need to know?

I spoke freely with Mom this morning from eight until ten-thirty a.m. and sang to her. I was half asleep, but it felt good to be able to speak freely to her.

Chantelle brought us a pizza and calzone for lunch, such a loving gesture.

I sat with Mom from four to six p.m. She is groaning every minute for thirty seconds and then the next thirty seconds she is quiet or without breath. Early on she blinked her left eye to me, as if to say, "Don't worry and don't take all this death stuff too seriously!" It really helped me.

I had always feared her death, not knowing how I would speak to her, but I seemed to be able to do that today and I feel satisfied that she heard me in some way. I truly believe that Mom has been waiting until she was sure there was some spiritual transfer to me so I would know that she'd be with me and since that has happened, now she can go on. During these past few days I wanted her to stay alive and in this extreme place I wasn't ready to let her go, but now I am ready.

I'm singing and speaking to her now and it seems to soothe her.

I told her whenever the time is right she can go on because now I truly believe that she is in my heart forever and I will be all right.

The wind is blowing outside. It sounds so cold.

## Wednesday, December 14, 1988 (nearly Midnight)
## "GOING HOME"

The dream I had a few days ago when I thought I was my mother dying, felt like we had merged in some way and sym-bolically it was that mother part of me that was dying. I knew she wondered if I would be all right without her. In this dying process, she and I were separating, but before we competed that separation it was as if she downloaded her internal files to me as represented by the knowing of her recipe. It was this assurance that allowed me to finally let go.

Within the energy of the celestial door opening wider, I accessed creative abilities I had never experienced before. I never thought I was an artist but my drawings of her just flowed out of me. I never before wrote a song in my life, but here, listening to the rhythm and drone of her death rattle, while at times feeling submerged in its deafening sound, I was given a song that we asked to be sung at her funeral service.

Where was all this knowing and creativity coming from? From my own soul bathed in the light pouring in. The experience is beyond words but I will attempt to describe it.

> Waves coming in—not quite light—pouring in—flood-ing the room like the smell of roses permeates every inch—
> as if we were submerged in a dense water—a thick substance—
> that still allows you to breathe—
> but this holy water fills the room like water would fill a fish tank—
> this room is without walls—you know the edges of it by the darkness.

I wanted more than anything to be with her at her time of death and she agreed that she wanted me with her, too and yet that night of December 14, I was distracted. I was in the kitchen sitting at the table as if detained from going into the next room to be with Mom. Then, right at midnight December 15, the doorbell rang. A woman who was supposed to give respite that night arrived and I ran down the two flights of stairs to release her from her shift, then ran back up to wake Chip as he had fallen into a deep sleep.

I believe now Mom needed those minutes to begin to go without me holding her back. I was blessed to experience her final breaths as Chip and I each held one of her hands and I breathed that last breath with her.

She breathed out...and then silence...I inhaled and broke our dance.

## Thursday, December 15, 1988 (5 a.m.)
## "THE GIFT OF DYING"

Mom went home to her true essence of being tonight at 12:40 a.m.

I was fully conscious and awake. I am so grateful she gave us the gift of dying in our presence.

When does death occur? It is customary to identify death when the heart and breath stops. Yet the soul is still hovering. So we stayed with her body. Some people may choose to bathe the body at this time as an honoring of that precious form, while releasing any energetic attachments from the body.

Marlene joined us and we had a beautiful send off for Mom. Chip and I read inspirational passages and I lit some incense. We sat with Mom and prayed and reminisced about her and her life, and Marlene was our witness.

I feel so taken care of by Mom. She stayed alive until we all were really ready for her to go—to release—to move on.

We called the funeral home and both men who came were dressed in suits and ties and it seemed appropriate that they did so as they were carrying our precious possession.

I must sleep now. Chip and I sat up writing the obituary and speaking about who we would choose to be the pall bearers.

It's five after five a.m. and Mom is having a party with Dad, Bob, Grandma, Uncle Mike, Uncle John, Uncle Sam, Uncle Joe, Mark, Uncle Anthony and all the other lovely souls. They are happy to see her. They've missed her, and are proud of the work she's done.

# Mother of Mine

Patricia Gulino Lansky

# Post Script

After Mom's death, when it was all over, I realized that my time of caregiving was one of the times I felt the most alive in my life. I had a singleness of purpose. I knew what I wanted to do and systematically did it, even though it was difficult at times.

I suppose this practice could be compared to training for and then running a marathon. That's what my caregiving sometimes felt like. I needed to endure, to keep my eye on the goal, and keep on keeping on.

So in the end, I not only missed her terribly, I also missed my role. I missed the clarity and focus of my caregiving as well.

"This is the true joy in life, being used for a purpose recognized by yourself as a mighty one. Being a force of nature instead of a feverish clod of ailments and grievances complaining that the world will not devote itself to making you happy...I want to be thoroughly used up when I die, for the harder I work the more I love."

George Bernard Shaw

For weeks, her final breath revisited me. I'd lay down to sleep and I'd hear her exhale and then I'd wait—wait for the inhale that never came. It was as if I was releasing that exhale with her, and there was no inhale in response.

I touched into that deepest stillness, that emptiness of the space after the last breath, and it terrified me. My falling asleep at night was filled with this peering into, falling into, this abyss... Then I would gasp and my inhale would wake me up again.

None of what happened affected me as much as the loss of that final inhale. The loss was deafening in the scream of nothingness. She's gone, it's done. Panic seized me each time.

I heard the lack of sound again and again. Mercifully, even that eventually stopped.

I wondered, as I continued to play back those final moments, "Was it my way of keeping her alive, to re-visit, review those details?" But no, it had a life of its own. I'd close my eyes and the scene would roll up to the awful final exhale. And then my panic would seize me again.

Those nights, or was it months, after her death, alone and quaking, took more courage than all of what I'd been through with her previously.

After her death and funeral, my brother and I went through the house deciding what we wanted to take and came across a box that Mom saved little mementos from our birthday parties, the candle holders, cards, etc. I cried as so many memories of happy times when she was young came flooding back. She had carefully saved those sentimental things for us, too. We gave what we didn't want from the house to an estate collector and drove to my brother's home. We wanted to be with our family for Christmas.

The drive felt as if we were being carried all the way. We drove east and the roads were dry on that December night and the huge full moon rose and illumined our way for hours. It was directly in front of us, beaming so much light we could see as if it were day. We couldn't miss the shining presence of our Mother, who had always been so in love with the moon, now expressing her overarching care and protection for us on our journey. We felt such comfort, such peace.

The next day there was a December snowstorm that would have made our travel impossible, but by then we were warm and safe in my brother's and sister-in-law's home with my nephew and Christmas all around us.

## What to Expect?

One day quite out of the blue, my Mother asked her hospice nurse, "What should I be expecting to encounter?"

Marlene said, "Go towards the light."

Because of our culture's denial of death, many people, if not most people, get to this point in their dying process, and they don't have any idea of what to expect. Rarely, if ever, is death and dying spoken about.

In essence, there is absolutely nothing to be afraid of in dying. Even though everyone's death is as unique as they are, it is possible to relax during it. You can drift down into greater levels of letting go, just like we do when we fall asleep or go into meditation. It seems that because the heart is slowing down, the outer extremities release circulation bit by bit, until the heart finally stops.

Dying is the opposite bodily experience of being born. The unborn fetus must be feeling an increased surge of energy in its body as the heart increases in strength. Perhaps that's why mothers feel the child kicking. Could these kicks be spurts propelled by bursts of energy and greater circulation?

Death and birth have transformation in common. In both, you are moving from one state to a completely different state, like ice transforming into water, and water transforming into steam. The chemical makeup of $H_2O$ is still the same in all three states, but expressed as different forms. It's just like the human being, first in the form of a fetus, then a person, and then a released soul.

How can transformation of form be understood? It is simply a miracle that cannot be accomplished through human will or human engineering. But we can co-create the transformation in concert with Spirit. Spirit is present in every step of our process. Transformation is like the stages of a butterfly. It begins as a caterpillar in a cocoon and miraculously, at some point, the furry worm transforms into a magnificent butterfly. Can we explain it? Not really. The caterpillar becomes a completely different form, enters into a completely different state. And that is exactly what happens in dying.

As souls released from our bodies, we lay down our bodies like an outfit discarded on the floor that goes limp when we step out of it. There is no longer any pain. The descriptions of the afterlife, by those who have had near-death experiences, confirm the sense of being in deep peace and pure joy, feeling indescribable beauty that fills one with ecstasy.

Some people report moving down a tunnel toward a magnificent light and seeing relatives and friends who have passed, greeting them and guiding along the path.

There is nothing to fear in dying. It is as natural and normal as breathing, as natural as being born. Through my own journey I have come to know that I am never alone; that none of us is ever alone. The Divine Presence is always with me, nearer than my heart beat. My wish for you is to be ever aware of a loving presence enfolding you, as well.

Sometimes what impedes our dying is our fear of letting go, especially because we may be frightened of not knowing what to expect. Perhaps some "final words" from some famous people will assure us of the beauty that awaits us.

Robert Louis Stevenson (author) "If this is death, it is easier than life…"

Vespasian (a Roman emperor from 69AD–79AD) "Dear me! I must be turning into a god…"

Beethoven (who was deaf) "I shall hear in heaven…"

William Hunter (a leading Scottish anatomist and physician 1718–1783) "If I had the strength to hold a pen, I would write down how easy and pleasant it is to die..."

Thomas Edison (inventor) "It is very beautiful over there..."

Steve Jobs (founder of Apple Computer) "Oh, wow, wow, wow!"

Dying and our afterlife is our next big adventure and no one should have to traverse that plateau in fear. Remember, you are not now, nor are you ever alone. You will certainly be well taken care of through your next miraculous transformation.

## What to Expect in the Time Leading up to Death

Here is a summary of what you might expect in the months and weeks leading up to your loved one's death, based on information in a pamphlet distributed by the National Hospice and Palliative Care Organization.

**The Final One to Three Months before Death: Withdrawing From Life.**

- Separating from the world.
- Not wanting to have visits from friends, neighbors, and sometimes family members.
- Decreased appetite and weight loss.
- Sleeping more and letting go of activities they used to enjoy.
- Lack of eating and drinking. This is not hurtful to the person because the body assists by producing a mild sense of euphoria at this time. It was a relief to know that my Mother was not suffering by not eating.
- Reminiscing and sharing old memories and contemplating their life. A life review process may be encouraged. They may use this time to make amends.

**One to Two Weeks before Death: The Veil is Lifting between This Life and the Next.**

- Sleeping most all of the time.
- Disorientation and changes in perception may occur.
- End of life hallucinations—the person may see or speak to people who aren't there. Sometimes these are people who have already died.
- They may pick at their sheets in a state of agitation.

- Movements and actions that may make no sense to others.
- Body temperature lowers.
- Blood pressure lowers.
- Pulse may slow down or become irregular.
- Skin color may change as circulation slows down.
- Breathing changes often becoming more rapid and labored.
- The extremities may feel cold to the touch.
- Speaking decrease and finally stops.

## A Couple of Days to Hours before Death: The End of This Earthy Walk.

- It is not uncommon for there to be a brief surge of energy near to death. (My father's experience was a clear example of this. Twenty-four hours before he died, he was very energetic and laughing with my Mom and the nurses, as I described. This surge of energy in others might be less noticeable.)
- Breathing is slower and there may be periods of rapid breathing followed by spaces of no breathing at all.
- Sometimes there is loud, rattling breathing from congestion in the airway. It said that the last sense to go is hearing, so it is helpful to sit and talk with your loved one at this time.
- Finally, breathing will stop and so does the heart. Death has occurred.

# SACRED PROCESS

## WHAT MEANING DO YOU ATTACH TO DEATH?

We have a deep reservoir of transformative power within us and a great part of that power is housed in the beliefs that we hold and the meaning we choose. Many of us are familiar with the idea that what we think and believe often manifests in our lives. For example, if we believe we are not worthy to be in a committed relationship, even though we say that we want to be in one, that unexpressed belief may be reflected in the lack of or trouble with intimate relationships in our lives.

At the level of healing in this mental realm, it is important to discover what the underlying meaning of your loss is to you, and to put it into words. To examine your deepest thoughts in this way is to recognize how death has created limitations in you so that you can let go of them and move forward.

Sometimes grief can hang on for what seems like an eternity. "Experts" used to say that there was a usual or ideal amount of time to grieve, but they have rescinded that concept because the timeline of grief is as individual as every person's sensitivity, quality of relationship with the deceased and accumulation of other losses in life. Therefore, while we may feel that our period of grieving is going on too long, is still too raw, there is no prescribed or "normal" length of time for grieving.

My personal period of grief was lengthy. Most times, when I sat down to write about my family losses, I found myself crying as if the thin scab of healing had been torn off my heart. I felt as if I was losing my loved one again, in that very moment, as I re-lived the loss over and over. This made the process of writing very difficult and depleting. I began to ask myself what was holding this raw grief in place.

A friend witnessing my ongoing, grief consoled me with her gentle words, "It doesn't have to be so hard. Go with what gives you life." This suggestion opened a whole new possibility for me. When the hurt surfaced as I wrote, I used that affirmation, *It doesn't have to be so hard.* I visualized the most supportive person I could imagine being with me during those bouts of grief. Little by little they lessened, and then the most amazing thing happened. Once I put my ideas into words and typed the memories onto the computer, the grief lost its charge. Could my grief have had the purpose of remaining in me until I could release it in this book? Did my past grief need to be exposed to the light of my present understanding of what I know now about the eternal soul?

Certainly, the seeds of this new, more expansive thinking were present in my experience of the final days with my mother. The dream I had of dying in her bed clarified the belief I held, "If you die—I will die." Clearly, I was losing more than my mother, as significant as that was. I was also losing the most supportive person in my life at that time. With both her and Bob gone, I was losing my sense of security, losing the wisdom of my elders. Who would I be without them?

In my final days with Mom, other seeds of understanding were planted in me. The creativity that surfaced showed that I had abilities that I had not yet tapped into. My re-creation of Mom's scalloped potatoes meant that her essence was not lost. I had not really lost her since her thoughts, beliefs and actions lived on in my memories of her.

I tell you all this as an example of why it is important to ask yourself what else you feel you are losing with the loss of your loved one. Is it a companion, best friend, confidant, your couple-ness, routine, hopes and dreams, feeling of immortality, innocence, your history, support, faith and trust, or something else? Be as specific and thorough as you can in exploring the full meaning of your loss. If possible, record your thoughts in a journal.

Do you have a friend or family member that you care about but, for whatever reason, you don't see each other or even communicate with anymore, yet you feel that your relationship with that friend still exists? Do you believe that after being apart, however long, you could pick up right where you left off as if there had been no time or distance between you? It's the same with loved ones who have died. You might find yourself thinking about them, hear their voice or laugh, remember how they walked or clothes they wore. Through all your knowing of the person, your relationship can continue to evolve. In the mind of our heart, we really all are connected because in the heart, there is no time or distance. Because there was love between you, your souls are expanded, filled with light and beauty and this magnificent energy remains in our souls for all eternity. No matter where you are, no matter where your loved one is—in the next room, in a distant country, in the spirit realm in one of the "many mansions"—the love, the connection remains.

To help in your healing process, recall vivid memories of your loved ones: funny things they said or did; special foods they made or enjoyed; talents or preferences; travels they took or you took together; physical features and ways in which you resemble them; whatever comes to mind about their uniqueness. Record these recollections in your journal.

# CHAPTER 7

# Developing a Practice of Letting Go

"Come to me, all of you, who are tired from carrying heavy loads and I will give you rest."

— MATTHEW 11:28

"If you suffer, it is not because things are impermanent. You suffer because you believe things are supposed to be permanent."

— THICH NHAT HANH, VIETNAMESE BUDDHIST TEACHER

WHY DO I highlight "letting go" above all other practices as a way to embrace life? The ability to let go, our level of ease with it, is the very process we must embrace as we die. In accepting death, we let go of our world, everything we have known, our loved ones, even our own body. Everything goes except for our soul, the lessons learned and the love we have given and received. Throughout life, each loss, each release is an opportunity to reassess how far we've progressed in our willingness to let go.

## The River

When I was five years old, I remember a special summer when my family was visited by our adult cousins who lived in Gary, Indiana. This was my first meeting with those handsome, towering people. It surprised me that these extraordinary beings were part of my family and they instantly loved me just because I was one of them. I delighted to be in their presence because they included me as if they'd always known me.

We all went to visit our other cousins in East Aurora, a fitting name for such a magical destination. On that hot summer day, we all changed into our bathing suits and laughingly cavorted on our way to the river behind my cousin's farm.

I hadn't yet learned how to float so Dad said he'd teach me. I remember the cousins' comforting presence with their playful ways surrounding me in the river. Dad held me on my back in the deeper middle of the river. I felt the slow flow of water on either side of me. I feared a bit as I tried to find the right place for my head—not under water, and not held above the water. I felt my Dad's hands supporting me, his calming voice talking to me. I didn't know how to make myself float, but then I felt it: the ever present support of the water. I just leaned back and I was carried effortlessly. The branches of the trees above me filtered streams of light through the leaves and the clear river filled with light rays as well.

When I found that place inside me of trust, in an instant I was floating.

It seemed so easy. Now I would never not know how to float. I wondered why I had been afraid of it before. I trusted my father to keep me safe and I relaxed into trusting the river to hold me and carry me. I couldn't get enough of lying on my back and gliding in the soft flow of that river. What a day it was—the day I learned to lie back, let go, and trust.

Can I remember to continue to relax into trusting the flow of my spiritual journey, of my unconditionally loving divine parent, who is even more sustaining and ever present than my dear father and those astonishing cousins could be? Yet all of their love was an expression of the eternal love, a love which released such joy in me.

## The Tibetan Buddhist Sand Mandala

If you ever have the opportunity to witness the construction of a Tibetan Buddhist Sand mandala, it is not to be missed. Creating a mandala is an ancient form of art and spiritual practice in which a team of Tibetan Buddhist monks use a variety of colored grains of sand to create a graphic and symbolic pattern in the form of a circle. They begin by drawing the outline of the design and then add various colors of sand to create one section at a time, working from the center outward.

We invited the construction of a Sand Mandala at our center and hundreds of people came, many with children, to watch the slow, methodical process of seven Tibetan monks piling grain after grain of sand into an intricate, three dimensional pattern. During the five days it took to complete the design, everyone who entered this sacred space was respectful and even little children were quiet. The only sound was the gentle scraping of the small metal tubes and funnels the monks used to apply the sand.

One of the days, I happened to be near a little boy sitting on his mother's lap, totally enthralled with the mandala process. The lad was told that as soon as the mandala was finished, the monks would destroy it.

"Why are they destroying it?" The boy found this incomprehensible.

One of the monks whispered, "It's about impermanence."

We adults nearby wondered how to explain impermanence to a five year old. My husband, Don, came to the rescue. "Nothing lasts forever. You know, it's like your toys. Sometimes they break. Sometimes you might not want them anymore."

As the little boy seemed to quietly mull that over, I wondered what lasting impression this mandala experience might have on his young mind. I wondered what impression our experience of an artistically created ritual of "nothing lasts forever," would make on each of our minds.

There is an old tale about a monkey who loved sweets. One day he discovered a jar half-filled with the special hard candy that he loved so much that he drooled over it. The monkey put his hand into the jar and grabbed a handful of candy, but with his fist full, he couldn't pull his hand out of the jar. If he could have let go of his attachment to having all those sweets at once, he might have eased one piece out at a time. Instead, in order to pull his fist out, he had to let go of all of it.

We may be afraid that when we let something go, nothing will take its place. We dread that what we lose will never be replaced with something at least as good, and certainly not better than what we have been holding onto so tightly. We fear the unknown and cling to that which is familiar. We can release these limiting beliefs and choose to believe that what is coming next can be better than what was before. To release in a positive and freeing way we can:

- recognize our attachment
- face it
- let it go
- be open to the possibility of having something better or becoming something greater.

At the end of the week of the Sand Mandala construction, we were told that the heart of Buddhism is contained in this ceremony which reinforces our wisdom and understanding that nothing is permanent. Appreciating change, we can see that from moment to moment, nothing is the same. We are encouraged through this ritual to let go and be at peace with releasing, not to dwell in the sadness of the loss, but to be open to the freshness of looking forward to what's coming next.

After some prayers and Tibetan chants, the Rinpoche, or head teacher, destroyed the mandala as soon as it was finished with one wave of his arm. Then his monks swept it up into a pile and placed it into an urn. This intricately designed and colorful art suddenly became just brown-gray dirt. Because part of the ritual includes disposing of the sand remains in a body of moving water, we caravanned to the river. I chose not to dwell in the melancholy sadness of loss, but remain open to the mystery of what would be next.

At the river, the seven monks stood in a line at the water's edge. They began their traditional chanting along with the deep sounds of the long Tibetan horns. They prepared to bless and infuse the water with the positive energies from the sacred sand. For them, the water symbolizes the home of all creatures and the origin of all life.

Amazing things began to happen. The little fish in the river who are usually so disinterested in anything other than their own swimming patterns, seemed to pause, line up to face the shore and stare at the monks.

Then with the crescendo of chants and horns blaring, four yellow butterflies went wild circling the monks. Finally, as the Rinpoche began to pour the sand into the river, a large dragonfly made his entrance parading in front of the monks. The day was alive with sun and clarity of air and sky, full of life-giving energy. All of us were blessed and I experienced the joy of being with what might be next. As beautiful as the mandala was, the releasing was in some ways even more beautiful.

In general, our Western culture doesn't teach us how to understand and relate to impermanence. In our culture, when a loss occurs we usually think that it shouldn't have happened, that something is wrong with its happening. Whether the loss is a divorce, or the loss of a job, or a death, we question it. Friends are often surprised when someone gets a divorce and both spouses are much happier after their decision to split up. Clearly, change and loss are not necessarily negative.

Most of us are not very comfortable with change. We prefer stability. And when the life we knew is swept away by illness or loss, we can feel adrift, confused, afraid, wanting to hold onto the life that's no longer there. These feelings are often difficult to deal with.

What if we practiced "dying daily?" To die daily, we must first notice and accept the loss or change, and then grieve what the loss or change means to us. Even a "happy" change, like moving from our present location to a new home, may present something we need to mourn and adjust to.

To die daily is to willingly let go of what no longer serves our expanding life. We have the ability to release on every level. On the physical level, we recycle clutter and old items from our environment and eliminate waste from our bodies. On the mental level, we release antiquated beliefs and limiting thoughts. On the behavioral level, we replace negative habits and patterns of behavior with more positive ones. As we release, we open to a new and healthier life. It is the practice of letting go, of surrendering to what is, of releasing the unnecessary, and worn-out, which brings rest and peace. It can be a practice, and a prescription for a fuller, freer life.

So we can choose to die daily—noticing the loss, grieving it, asking for a new vision of larger meaning over all of it, and finally releasing it to the All. This practice grows us and provides us with a happier life. In dying daily we become scrubbed clean of the past, opening ourselves to a boundless future. We overcome death by choosing to live.

## Gladys

There can be something really pleasant in having a mother-in-law. It certainly was for me. I found in Gladys the love and support of a mother without any baggage of childhood associations with her. Ours was an easy relationship of mutual respect and genuine affection.

Gladys was intelligent, well read, and loved to talk with people. All of this prepared her well to maintain her own home as a popular Bed & Breakfast and there she forged many lasting friendships. People enjoyed being with her and delighted in her dry sense of humor.

I loved to hear the exquisite tones of her grand piano in the morning. Her touch was so sensitive and expressive. Her sound was unique, and she could have been a concert pianist but for life's interruptions. She loved and took great care of her piano, a gift from her husband long ago. The piano was an expression of who she was.

Gladys' body did not keep up with her lively mind, and physical deterioration continued into her late seventies resulting in the need for kidney dialysis. This was difficult for her. My husband and I felt frustrated and even somewhat guilty at living so far away from her that we couldn't offer her as much help as we would have liked.

Eventually, after giving the dialysis a very good run for about one and a half years, her body was just too tired to go on, and Gladys made the decision to stop treatments. She knew, as we did, that it would be a brief two or three days before the toxins would fill her body and claim her life. No one blamed her for her decision. It was not arrived at lightly, but only after her quality of life had become unbearable. As the body gets to such a worn out state, it knows when it's time to let go of life.

Gladys didn't care about having a funeral. She said it was up to us if we wanted one. My husband and his brother and niece and I decided on an open house reception on a summer afternoon held at her Victorian home in Maine a week after her death. In preparation, the four of us went through innumerable boxes of photos, albums and slides of Gladys' life. I realized there was so much I never knew about her and the family. One thing was clear; Gladys had been a radiant beauty in her youth. Her face was captivating and regal. At the final gathering we displayed many of the old photos on the top of her piano. It was perfect watching all the people mill around Gladys' piano. We served lots of food and so many friends came and reminisced and shared their love of her with us and with each other.

## THE PIANO

She told me once how nearly fifty years ago
her newlywed husband took her shopping
to find a piano.
This stunning, talented young bride
tried each one and finally heard
a particular mellow brilliance—
    *her* piano.

The piano became the centerpiece of life
and a cradle of sound for both her young sons.
Playing underneath it, Gladys' music
inspired them to act out all that their imaginations heard.
One son was drawn to play the piano
and music of his heart overflowed
    directly into his hands.

How many times did Gladys play her piano in this lifetime?
Imagine
repeated and loving touches
giving life to this silent object,
the piano becoming an extension of her soul,
touch upon touch upon touch,
    sounding uniquely of her.

When she died,
and movers came to dismantle the piano,
its magnificent musical body went silent.
Finally disassembled
into portable pieces,
it released her soul from its heart.
    Witnessing it, we wept.

Patricia Gulino Lansky

Because the piano reassembled perfectly,
we were taken by surprise
that it no longer sounded like Gladys.
Now,
in its new home,
it resonates in tune with
    the loving heart of her son.

## The Scattering

Gladys didn't ask for much in her end-times, but she did request that her ashes be scattered in the ocean. Of course we would fulfill her last wish, but how? There was no bridge over the part of the ocean where we were. It seemed strange and awkward to stand at the beach and try to toss ashes into the ocean. A neighbor came to the rescue. He offered to take us on his boat through the inlet into the broad ocean. We were so grateful for his thoughtfulness.

We four, her two sons, one granddaughter and I, took a circuitous route by car with our neighbor John to a cottage that housed his little boat. We left from the dock, moving slowly through the cove until the motor started to act up. John was worried that if we went as far into the ocean as we had planned, we might not get back. Instead, we idled where we were, in the most picturesque Maine inlet that flows out to the sea. Despite our concern about the fragility of that little boat, Gladys' scattering became a mystical experience. One I will never forget.

Her older son offered a prayer beginning with a paraphrase from Emerson.

> We are all Stardust
> and are turned into the All that is all.
> Mom, you are now one with all of life.
> You are part of this ocean and all that is.
> I now forgive all and bless all and release you to your
> ongoing good.
> The light of God surrounds you,
> the love of God enfolds you,
> the power of God protects you,
> the presence of God watches over you.
> Wherever you are, God is.

As we four remaining descendants balanced in the back of the boat, holding the box of her ashes, did we really know what he meant when he said she is now "one with all?" Was she "one" with the beauty of the cove where we idled, with the old pines standing sentinel on the rocky cliffs to our right? "One" with the water that was everywhere—as the ocean, and as the mist dripping from the gray sky, covering our heaviness in the bracing cool air?

The dancing wind played with the first handful of her ashes and lifted them in all directions, like an offering to the gods. The fine dust spray covered us—dust on our slickers, on our faces. *We* were one with Mom! As we leaned over the edge of the boat to pour the rest into the wake, to see the water rise and swell to catch her, the very wave of her streaming behind us, her ashes made the water grow in volume. The lighter gray ash became a huge mammal, like a newborn dolphin or a whale swimming along, trailing behind our boat, breathing in new life and new freedom. Released from the confines of the black plastic box into the ocean, Gladys grew larger. I glimpsed her magnificent, unbounded, eternal soul, and she became even greater in my sight as she retreated from us. I wept at the beauty of her new form and that we were letting her go, releasing her, giving her away.

A part of me wanted to hold onto those bits of ash as if, in holding on, I might bring her back. But then, that great gray leviathan dove deep into the sea, and I literally heard the words of the prayer as her essence permeated the ocean. "You are part of this ocean, and all that is." Gladys was filling the cove but not stopping there. She was swimming the world, covering the seven oceans, seeing again all the exotic places she had been and all the others she had wanted to see.

I hear her in the dark night air that lifts the curtains and rattles the bedroom door. "Are you here, Mom?" Of course she is. She is One with all.

"Take good care of my son."

"Yes, I will."

I hear her love in many places; in the remarks of friends; in the showering of her bequests; in the tears of my heart; in deeper love than I was aware of until now; in her "Victorian Lady," her home that I don't want to leave, knowing that I may never be here again. I try to hold on to her physical surroundings and possessions because in some way they feel more real. Then I understand that the love, allowing me to have a second chance, to be a part of another mother-daughter pair—this second time, as daughter-in-law, a little easier—that was the most real of all.

As with other loved ones no longer with me, in that aching emptiness that sears my heart, I wish there had been more—more time, more connection, more history, more parts of her life known. That is when I hear, "Pass the love forward, pass it on," so that in the coming times, when so many others will also be scattered in the wind, flowing into their own custom-designed and eternal journey, I can say, "I knew them well. I loved them well."

## Trusting the Mystery

How do thousands of people make sense of the shocking loss of their homes through the many recent natural disasters of fire or flood or storm? Many have lost every possession, every photograph of their history. All of it had meaning to them. Yet many say, "I'm just so grateful that my family is still alive."

They choose to see the situation in a larger context. They create a bigger container in which to hold the meaning of their life and experience. They realize that previously their life meant "having my prized possessions with me." They have stepped onto the upward spiral of life and said, "I value life more than all these lovely, often precious and sometimes expensive possessions. I may miss them, but my life is blessed because my family survived."

I used to mourn to varying degrees the loss of all that is impermanent: people, happiness, the last bite of the dark chocolate bar, youth, the body, innocence, friends, position, play, work, a perfect day, the colored leaves, the sweet cover of sleep, all these and more. Any loss can be sad even intensely sad, at times. Impermanence is just the way our world is constructed. It is not good or bad. It is just what exists.

Yet, if we place one impermanence next to another, something can lift. If I pair sadness with happiness, I become so grateful that sadness doesn't last forever even while I concede that happiness is ephemeral as well. If I pair the pain and agony of my loved ones' bodies invaded with cancer with their mortality, I can accept that they are time limited on this earth, and I am grateful their pain doesn't last forever. When I consider all the many things that I'm relieved to know are impermanent, like evil, suffering, natural disasters, mistakes, confusion, anger, hatred, then I am also willing to let go of all the good that I must release as the things I love fade away.

Yet love itself never dies because love given and love received changes our very soul into something more expanded. The only thing we will take with us when we leave this earthly plane is our soul filled with all the learning and loving of a lifetime. Love leaves tender prints on our soul. Let love change us. Let love grow our arms, extending them in a welcoming embrace of all that is just the way it is.

## Ministry

Supporting people during life's transitions is one of the privileges and blessings of ministry. Over the years my husband and I, as co-ministers, have seen the fullness of life in all of its variations and witnessed many deaths but I am choosing to focus on three very different men who each had what I refer to as radiant deaths.

The first man, I'll call him Peter, actively worked to apply spiritual principles in his life. His lifetime of searching served him well in his final days when he shared with family and friends that he wasn't afraid to die. Peter had absolute certainty that we are all intended for something much greater and that he would be experiencing that soon. As I visited with Peter a short time before he died, he was so at peace in his faith. He spoke of an experience of angels that surrounded him and comforted him and told him it wasn't his time quite yet. Their presence and assurance lifted Peter into a clearly visible, radiant state of grace. He glowed from within in quiet bliss.

The second man, I'll call Ed. Ed shared his dying with me for nearly the last two years of his life as he received treatments for cancer. He worked to put his life in order and to come to an understanding and resolution of the questions and mysteries of his life. It was an honor to share this journey with him. Ed was also a deeply spiritual person, a man of great dedication and service to his church and the people around him. He saw himself as a peacemaker. We spoke two weeks before his death and Ed talked about experiencing the Light, the heavenly realm. He felt the other world was warm, comforting and soothing. He felt a calming presence within himself and knew he had nothing to fear.

He told me that he had visited heaven on three occasions before the Saturday when he moved there for good. He said he experienced a great sense of peace and contentment there. It was vividly real but at the same time hard to understand. He learned something more from each visit and he was hoping there would be more. We'll never know if there were more because he was too close to death to carry on a conversation with us.

Ed said that while there, he was surrounded by many lights, each one with a different hue. Together they made a mosaic of lights resembling a wall that surrounded him. He noticed on a later visit that some of the lights moved while he was still and when they did, it became clear to him that they were beings and that behind them was a brighter light that he felt was God. He said there was a familiarity about some of these beings but that he did not recognize anyone. It seemed that there was a sense of learning with each visit, and he hoped that more time would reveal more understanding. Throughout our two years of sharing, we spoke about going to the light at death and, when I saw Ed the night before he died, he was peacefully lying in bed with his eyes closed. I leaned over close to his ear and whispered, "Remember to go toward the light." He opened his eyes wide and with mouth pursed he emphatically whispered, "I'm there. I'm in the light."

All the rites of passage of people we have come to know and love never fail to evoke a mixture of happiness and tears. One such time juxtaposed the emotional opposites all in a single night.

Chidambar, not his real name, is also one I deeply cherish. I chose the name Chidambar to respect the privacy of his family. For me, the meaning of this name is a perfect expression of this beautiful soul. Chidambar means one whose heart is as vast as the sky.

He shared with us some of his earlier years. His entire family experienced displacement and loss as a result of the tumultuous Partition of India by the British Indian Empire on August 15, 1947. It is estimated that 14 million Hindus, Sikhs and Muslims were displaced during the partition; it was the largest mass migration in human history.

In later years, Chidambar became an important part of our spiritual community as a revered elder. Some called him "a saint." Although he had little means, he was enormously generous with whatever he had. Every Sunday, he would bring a bouquet of flowers for the altar, whether the service had started or not. This was his honoring ritual and no matter where we were in the service, we would always stop and allow him to say his silent prayer and bow before he placed the flowers on the altar.

People were always warmly welcomed at his efficiency apartment to share some tea, a snack and time together. It was his custom to give some little gifts to the children of the community to commemorate the anniversaries of his wife's and Mother's birthdays. In complete trust, he'd hand us a blank check and order us to buy something for the children from him. We would protest spending his money, but when he persisted, we were always sure not to spend more than ten dollars.

Being well past ninety, and unconcerned about not knowing exactly how old he was, Chidambar didn't show any signs of illness. He was still mobile and active yet we noticed that he was gradually slowing down. Eventually, we were concerned to learn he had taken to his bed full time.

One Friday night, we conducted a wedding rehearsal at our center and on the way to the rehearsal dinner a block away from Chidambar's apartment, we took the opportunity to spend some time visiting him before attending the dinner.

As we peeked into his room, we found Chidambar, propped up in his bed fully awake and conscious with his assembled family completely filling the floor space around his king-sized bed. He greeted us and since there was no more room to stand in his small bedroom, he waved us to come onto his bed to be near him.

Slipping off our shoes, we crawled on the bed over to where he was lying. He looked as he always did, perhaps a bit thinner and a little tired. His son told us that he was bleeding a little but not in pain. We shared with Chidambar our plans for the evening and then he said, "Tell me, what I can give this couple as a gift for their wedding?"

We said, "No, that is not necessary. You don't know them. Don't give it another thought."

Here was a man close to death yet he was still thinking of others. A core practice of his life, he asked one more time, "How can I give? How can I be of service to another?"

We prayed with Chidambar and his family and against all professional decorum we broke down. We loved him so much. Our intention was to soothe him and here he was comforting us. I remember the deep sense of presence and compassion in his voice as he told us not to worry, that it was God's will.

Just two hours later, at the rehearsal dinner, we received the call that Chidambar had died peacefully with his loved ones surrounding him. We were told that his family circled his bed and as they stood together, Chidambar silently focused one at a time on each person, as his gaze went around the entire circle of his beloved ones. After connecting with the last person, he closed his eyes and died.

Here was an extraordinary man who devoted his life to God. He seemed to be intoxicated with God. He saw himself as a servant of God and practiced what he perceived to be God's will. His room had many pictures of master teachers that he had followed throughout his lifetime. He was well educated, yet always humble in every interaction. And even now, so many years after his death, people who knew him seem to never tire of telling loving stories about Chidambar still alive in their hearts.

These three men are not alone in the serene beauty of their dying. They showed us the possibility of dying in grace.

## CHERISHED ONES

This hospital room holds their father and her husband.
Keeping vigil they rearrange the sterile room into their cozy family space
placing memories of their life together near him,
their greatest treasure.

Her thin body fits next to his in that hospital bed.
Lips that have kissed
now only hers move in soothing words
sounds that touch him inside his silence
and envelop all in that room
with their endless love.

In a different room
she is fully present with her beloved and two friends.
"Please wash my hair today?"
And the women grateful to do for her
say "Yes."

So many caring and careful touches
as they lift her head off the pillow
into a bowl that's like an inflated beach toy
testing the temperature
they anoint her head with soft streams of water

blessings of gentleness
touch each one of them.
And her eyes
always blue-beautiful
now are liquid eyes—still alive
deep openings to her luminous soul.

Those with her match her delicacy.
The brush stroke in this final work of art is soft and slow.
Sweet smiles and murmurs of appreciation
as they dry her long, fond curls
and still those eye pools
consciously melt all of us
into tenderness.

Yes, in the end time
as the outer falls away
we are face to face with Beauty.
We bow in awe at the altar of each soul
in the presence of Truth revealed.

Let her, let him
press onto you—
a touch of softness
caring, lifting, transporting forevermore
each one of us.

## ONE LEAF

It's August.
Last night the cicadas' concert swelled
washed in the full moon light.

Mists awaken the morning.
The land, unable to hold it all,
breathes heavy moisture into the air.
Trees engorged in green
pulse with vibrant life.

In all this fullness,
                there—
one yellowed leaf
back-lit by sumptuous green,
sways its way down.

Even now, on this day of warm light
                the end
has its beginning.

Soon, sooner than we think,
dried leaves will be scattered
will be swept up,
piled,
gone.

May we become like that leaf
ready to let go
each time it is time
dancing lightly down
on the evergreen air.

## Humor: Letting Go Of Seriousness

"Once the game is over, the king and pawn go back into the same box."

Italian proverb

There is nothing better than being with good friends and family after a funeral. I was blessed to be with my brother and sister-in-law and our friend, Jay, the evening after we buried our Mother. Jay is an old friend who often expresses compassion through his actions and is as beautiful inside as outside. I deeply appreciated his company.

The four of us sat around Mom's kitchen table that night and told stories. The conversation began to move in a new direction when Jay told a story of inadvertently stepping on and sliding on a pizza. I don't remember the particulars, but I will never forget how hysterically funny it was. Each of us then took turns trying to top his recollection with their own funny stories. We were crying tears of laughter, and holding our sides in pain, a good pain this time.

For each of us, our laughter was a release of all we had been going through and a relief. It balanced the extreme seriousness of the situation with a shared lightness. We know that our Mom would've enjoyed these stories as much as we did. Mom had her own brand of humor. Even now, so many years after her death, whenever my cousin and I reminisce, we end up with belly laughs when we recall a particular turn of phrase or inflection for which Mom was famous. It always feel good to laugh with my cousin as we share memories of Mom.

Gladys, my mother-in-law, was also very funny. One time when she was in the hospital, an entourage of doctors and interns crowded into her room to discuss her case. It was so packed in there that she said, "Would you like me to step outside to give all of you more room?" And when she was asked near the end of her life, "What would you like your family to do with your ashes?"

She replied, "Oh, they can take them to a movie—hopefully not a horror flick."

Norman Cousins in *Anatomy of an Illness*, describes what he did when he was diagnosed with cancer. He decided to gather all his favorite comedy movies and he laughed his way to health. Laughter is a good medicine anytime, even in grief.

Here are some musings of others that you may find refreshing.

"Life does not cease to be funny when people die any more than it ceases to be serious when people laugh."

George Bernard Shaw

"I am ready to meet my Maker. Whether my Maker is prepared for the great ordeal of meeting me is another matter."

Winston Churchill

"Millions long for immortality who do not know what to do with themselves on a rainy Sunday afternoon."

Susan Ertz, *Anger in the Sky* (1943)

"Immortality: a fate worse than death."

Edgar Shoaff

"Death? Why this fuss about death? Use your imagination, try to visualize a world without death! Death is an essential condition of life, not an enemy."

Charlotte Perkins Gilman

"I'm always relieved when someone is delivering a eulogy and I realize I'm listening to it."

George Carlin

"According to most studies, people's number one fear is public speaking and number two is death. Death is number two! Does that sound right? This means to the average person, if you go to a funeral, you're better off in the casket than doing the eulogy."

Jerry Seinfeld

"Death should not be seen as the end but as a very effective way to cut down expenses."

Woody Allen

"My grandmother was a very tough woman. She buried three husbands. Two of them were just napping."

Rita Rudner

## THIS NEW SPRING

As we sit together, old friend,
encircled by this silent sanctuary of sunlight,
on this damp and delightful day,
we murmur memories of the heart,
of ghosts that neither wish to leave
nor do we wish to let them go.

How can we relinquish them
when such beauty, such meaning,
and pieces of our souls
inhabited those lost days?
What good can ever replace
what has been the best?

Beside us is the garden
poised in that exhalation
between dead of winter
and the first burst of spring.
We await its luscious perennial buds
to poke up irrepressibly
and open the surprise that arrives
new each year.

Weren't last year's blossoms fabulous?
Can nature top what was?
Time after time, again and again,
she releases her best work.
Then, as radiant pastel petals disappear,
does she bless them and shed a tear?

Patricia Gulino Lansky

May she teach us
that the most beautiful, the best
once let go
soon honors us with the new,
also beautiful, also best,
time after time
in this time
for this new spring.

# SACRED PROCESS

## THE PRACTICE OF LETTING GO

Why should we release and let go?

Think of it this way. What if we could never let go of any possession we ever received? Our homes would be filled up in no time with layers and layers of stuff from our earliest days to the present. Of course, there would be the sentimental items like the first baby shoes, but there would also be all those dirty diapers, as well!

From this extreme perspective, we can see that letting go is a powerful action of releasing what is no longer necessary. We release in order to create a clearing, an energetic vacuum for the new and fresh to be received. Stagnation, constriction, holding on are dead ends.

Life is flow. Change is good. Change brings new opportunities for learning, growth and relationships. Make room for the new by gently and gratefully saying goodbye to the no longer needed items and ways of the past.

Think of this practice like opening a window that has been closed for the long months of winter and can now let in the clean, fresh air of spring.

Below are four phrases which the Twelve Step program literature call their slogans that can serve to guide our practice of letting go. (The Twelve Step program is a spiritual path that suggests a course of action to recover from addiction, compulsion or other behavioral issues.)

## Slogans:

### LIVE AND LET LIVE

Let others live and choose their personal path. When we judge another's choices, we can remember to release criticism, and mind our own business. Focus on our own life and decisions. We will learn to be kinder to ourselves by being respectful of others and by releasing self-criticism.

### HOW IMPORTANT IS IT?

People don't have to be and do things the way we want them to. We can let go of our firmly held "shoulds"—how things "should" be, or how people "should" behave. Put things into perspective. In one hundred years will anyone care what style her dress was? What is really important?

### KEEP IT SIMPLE

Simplify your life. Release the unnecessary. Eliminate clutter and chaos. Underneath the "pack-rat" mentality may be a real fear of scarcity or not having enough. Perhaps you anticipate that once you throw away that sweater you've had since high school, the next week you will need that exact vintage item for some unforeseen reason.

Release this fear of scarcity and future regret by noticing and giving thanks for what the object provided you with in your life. If it still has use, donate it to some worthy cause. Bless it and your experience and affirm with a feeling of satisfaction that "I am so grateful that all my needs are so caringly addressed and provided for now and in the future."

Make it a practice to clear some area of your space for five to ten minutes each day. It could be a drawer, or a pile of papers, or a closet. Enjoy the new order and spaciousness.

LET GO AND LET GOD
We can get caught up in wanting to control things. We know that we are powerless over others in many ways, most especially those that we love.

We can practice trusting in their inner wisdom and also in the divine order and love of the universe. We can turn people and situations over to a Higher Power and affirm: "I know that Divine Love is always active in my life and in the lives of my loved ones regardless of what the momentary outer appearance may look like."

## Letting Go of Resentments

Forgiveness is an essential spiritual practice for cultivating a greater life. Holding onto anger and resentment is misdirected energy. The Buddha compared resentment to holding a hot coal in your hand with the intent to throw it at someone else. Meanwhile the coal is burning your own hand.

Make it a habit to review each day and ask yourself, "Am I at odds with anyone?"

Have I hurt anyone or has anyone hurt me in thought, word, or deed. Remember that the person you might be at odds with could be others, or yourself. Decide right then to release and let go of the "hot coal." Forgiveness doesn't mean condoning bad behavior. It just means that you are not willing to let it obstruct your happiness or allow it to have power over you. In the Twelve Step programs this is called making amends with each person in such a way that will not bring harm to yourself or anyone else. Amends can include apologies, restitution, or even making a commitment to yourself to eliminate behavior that is less than your best self.

Through forgiveness, your clear and resolved heart will welcome greater health, mental well-being, and increased self-esteem. The practice of daily forgiveness allows for a more peaceful death without a backlog of regrets at the end of life.

## Peering through the Veil

Contemplation and reflection on your life up to this point and beyond is an important process.

- What are the lessons of your life?
- What new skills and awareness have you developed?
- What do you intend to do with the time you have remaining?
- How would you like to be remembered?
- Do you choose to love more—yourself and others?

# Epilogue

A YOUNG BOY is the narrator of the classic novel, *A Death in the Family* by James Agee. The boy begins by recounting a summer evening with his family in 1915 in Knoxville, Tennessee. He is surrounded by the beauty of that time and place and by the love of his family. It is a time of innocence and peace before he experiences the reality of death. He ends the introduction with these words:

> and those [my family] receive me, who quietly treat me, as one familiar and well-beloved in that home: but will not, oh, will not, not now, not ever; but will not ever tell me who I am.

Why won't they tell him? Because no one can tell you who you are. You must discover it through your experiences, the lessons they teach you, and the help you are drawn to. You discover who you are by following your heart's yearnings, by asking and praying, and through mistakes, love, and grace.

Death not only made me question who I was, it also brought up many other complex, core questions, such as:

- Where is God in all of this?
- Why are we here?
- Are we really souls? Is there a part of us that endures?
- Why does God allow such pain and suffering?

In the process of being touched by death, you may discover your own answers to these and other questions and begin to create a deeper relationship with the God of your understanding. What I mean by God is whatever name or phrase rings true for you: Mother-Father God, Allah, Jesus, Buddha, Yahweh, Hashem, Spirit, Nature, the One, the Tao, the Allness of the Isness, Higher Power, Creator, Divine Being, Great Spirit; the list goes on and on.

The truth I have discovered is that we are all children of God; each of us is a manifestation, an out-picturing of our Creator/Parent. Therefore, as a "mini-me" of God, we have in potential all the attributes of our Divine Parent. We have waiting within us a full expression of love, life, imagination, wisdom, power, and much more. This is our true inheritance. We don't inherit nearly as much as from our earthly parents as we do from our heavenly parent who created us in its image. Shakespeare captured this in his play, *Hamlet* (Act 2, Scene 2):

"What a piece of work is man, [and woman], how noble in reason, how infinite in faculties; in form and moving how express and admirable, in action how like an angel, in apprehension [understanding] how like a god..." [all brackets mine]

I conceptualize my connection and relationship with God in this way: I am a wave in the ocean heart of God, made up of the same attributes and composition as the rest of the ocean. Like a wave, I arise from the depths of the ocean and extend into the air above the surface, rolling along with focus and mass for the time that is mine. Then at some point, and each wave is unique in this, I will run my course and merge back into the sea with whatever pebbles, or shells, or sand I gathered along the way. All of us carry our pieces of experience and learning back with us, having changed the earth we touched and been changed by all that occurred here.

Why are we here in this human body? Are we really spiritual beings having a human experience? From birth, life is a gradual process of knowing where we came from, but soon forgetting this essential truth. Suffering can facilitate remembering by opening our heart to know, as if for the first time, who we are. We can endure great hardships and become stronger because of them.

But why does God allow us to suffer? This could very well be the most often asked question because suffering is so universally part and parcel of our existence. That's both the bad news and the good news.

First of all, I suggest that you never buy into the misguided belief that we are suffering because we are being punished by an angry God. God is our unconditionally loving Spirit/Creator/Parent. Ask yourself if any loving human parent would ever *purposely* try to hurt his or her child? Of course not. How much more love than a human parent must God have? God is Love itself and God never has to forgive because God never condemns in the first place.

Knowing our oneness with Spirit that wishes only the highest and best for us puts everything in life into perspective. We no longer fear death, knowing that the continuum of life and our eternal home is in the loving heart of God. Albert Einstein said, "The most important decision we make is whether we believe we live in a friendly or hostile universe."

So why, then, do we have to experience pain? Change, conflicts, and challenges, are ultimately intended to bless us as we unravel the lessons we must learn and call forth the latent strengths and resources that are within us. We come to know that we have a resilient, overcoming nature and there is nothing in this world that has power over us to make us unhappy or destroy our peace. We learn that we have choice over how we interpret life's ups and downs. We can begin to see life and death in new ways, not restricted by what seems to have always been "just the way things are."

Have you ever been afraid of the volume of sadness inside you? Have you had the thought, "If I ever started crying I wouldn't be able to stop and my sadness would consume and obliterate me?" This is not an uncommon fear. I have had that fear. In my desperation I let myself cry it out and found that I came to a place of the end of those tears. I was exhausted and complete. I discovered that there is a part of me that is stronger than my sadness and I never again had to fear the uncontrollable outpouring of my tears.

Did you ever wonder why Jesus in his end days experienced so much pain that it is said he "sweat tears of blood?" At one point in the Garden of Gethsemane, Jesus did ask God to take away his pain but then he accepted his situation for he knew that the pain of the human condition was part of life. Jesus modeled for us that we can endure great hardship and can overcome our pain, just as he did. Jesus showed us how to transcend pain so completely by coming to the point of honestly forgiving the people who were killing him and said with compassion, "Father forgive them for they know not what they do." (Luke 23:34)

May we all know that even though terrible, painful things may happen to us, at the core we are eternal souls, and the soul can never be destroyed. May we find that no one and nothing, not even death, can defeat us. Nothing outside of us has the power to keep us from the goodness that awaits us. Only when we give our power away to another or to a situation can suffering overwhelm us.

We are designed for more than just this lifetime; we are souls for all eternity and the troubles of this brief lifetime are designed to expand our soul. All the lessons we learn, the challenges that come our way, the pain and loss endured are opportunities to become more compassionate and contributing beings. The more evolved we become as souls, the greater difference we can make in this world.

What if we could consciously move into our time of death with curiosity and anticipation of what we are about to experience? Will we find that we can put down all the trapping of this life and soar free of any constraints, without fear or regrets? Can we call complete whatever we have started in life, accepting that when we die everything we were meant to do in this lifetime has been completed in the most perfect way in alignment with a higher purpose?

Our greatest gift is to live life fully. One who is aware of the bigger picture of eternal life is free of the fear of the inevitability of death and can echo St. Paul:

"Death has been swallowed up in victory.
Where, O death, is your victory?
Where, O death, is your sting?"
1 Corinthians 15:54–55

Then death is no longer an enemy. There are no enemies left. Looking at death directly transcends fear. There is nothing to fear. (Remember the acronym F-E-A-R stands for False-Evidence-Appearing-Real.) What remains is a space of freedom and love.

I have come to see that there is a divine plan and a divine order in the universe. Who died and when they died is not ever by accident. The ones who died fulfilled their purpose here on earth, did what they needed to do, impacted people exactly the way they were supposed to. It was the right and perfect time for them to return to the spirit realm to continue as a soul without a body. This is true for everyone whether they lived one day or one hundred years.

When was the last time you looked, really looked at a diamond? Did you notice its crystal clarity; the cuts that allow even more light to emerge; the colors shimmering in it; the beauty of nature's creation? They can't be easily chipped, nicked, or broken.

How did diamonds get this way? Pressure. For eons the ordinary rock was squeezed and squeezed under tons of pressure so that now it is able to withstand the most extreme forces of nature and last forever. We are diamonds in the rough. Pounded by life and pain and suffering we finally come to know our own unrepeatable beauty and resilience.

Do you know the story of Jacob from the Hebrew Bible? (Genesis 32:24–31) This is one of my favorite stories. Jacob dreamed that he wrestled with an angel all night and said to the angel, "I won't let you go until you bless me." After the angel blessed Jacob he said, "For I have seen God face to face, and yet my life is preserved."

Pain and suffering continue to wrestle with us, forcing us to wake up, not letting us sleep in denial in the dark of night. This is how we can receive the blessings, the lessons of new personal growth and deepening awareness of who we really are and of what we are made, eventually discovering a place of total trust within us.

The pain that faces us through death and dying is tied to our own survival. Instead of seeing death as our enemy, as Jacob might have viewed this wrestling angel as his enemy, we can find death is our angel come to bless us in unimaginable ways. We all have an indomitable core. As an eternal soul we are invited to meet and wrestle with the Divine messages in difficult situations. In doing so we choose not to rest until, by overcoming our limitations, we discover how our suffering has become a blessing.

Then our suffering, betrayal and pain become our teachers so that we can learn compassion, trust and joy and ultimately through death we can learn to treasure life. The greatest darkness can reveal the truth of the Light that lives within us and as us.

Wrestle with your angel until you are blessed and transformed.

## FULL CIRCLE

It's almost over—
this endless humid summer day.
Finally, it's dusk.
In the quiet of the evening,
the air is still, unruffled

Then—
something catches my eye
Blink—there it is again—
A firefly! And then another and another
a concert of light individually played
from each quadrant of the lawn
      each in its own rhythm
      shining its own brilliance
bl—ink, blink, blink

The growing darkness holds these fleeting creatures
and they delicately remind me
      of the mystery,
      the presence
      of the unseen, magical
      Beingness that is within the darkness,
         beneath the surface of everything

Now it is full night.
The orchestral light-suite is finished
yet one final blink
      winks at me.
All is well.

# Acknowledgements

MY FAMILY IS the foundation of everything in this book. Starting with the permission my mother gave me when the idea first dawned that I might write a book about her, to my brother's encouragement to write about my many experiences with death and dying, re-kindling my commitment to do so, I was inspired by my family and by each one of their unique life stories.

From the bud of the idea in those early days, I am forever grateful to my life-long friend, Evelyn Brady who has been my Muse—always believing in this project and connecting me with the brilliant and compassionate editor, Julianna Ricci. As a partner in editing, Julianna's spiritual understanding, patience and clarity untiringly supported this work to completion. She is an answer to my prayers for the perfect editor for me to work with and our synergy fueled each other to work like lightening. The unwavering dedication and friendship of both women are beautiful gifts to me.

And to Jay Peterson who generously shared his amazing talents as a professional graphic designer transforming my thoughts about the cover into inspired artistic expression. I am deeply grateful to you for your love and creativity and enduring friendship.

Additional loving support came from: Laurie Farrington, Rev. Bil and Rev. Cher Holton, Rev. Jesse James, Blair Jones, Rev. Paula Mekdeci, Cynthia Moore, Rev. Mary Morrissey,

Eddie Oliver, Rev. Mary Omwake, Rev. Joyce Fisher Pierce, Rev. Richard Rogers, Rev. Barbara Jean Stannard, Jay and Susan Perry, Suzette Stewart, and Jan Triplett. During the 2014–2015 year, my poetry was encouraged by the accomplished poets in the Poetry Critique Group facilitated by Elizabeth Doyle Solomon, with Leonard Tuchyner, Sigrid Mirabella, and Linda Levokove. A multitude of thanks to all of you, my dear friends.

Gratitude to my spiritual family at Unity of Charlottesville. Your love and support is part of the greatest treasures in my life. It is my joy to know and love you.

Most of all I am deeply grateful to my beloved husband Don, who carries all my dreams in his generous heart and who gave several rounds of editing and endless support. He held me through my tears of grief and always provided me with "pens"—whatever was needed for my work to be made manifest. His clarity, brilliance, discernment, and beautiful love always bless me.

# Bibliography

Agee, James. *A Death in the Family.* New York: Bantam, 1957.

Atwater, PMH. *The Big Book of Near-Death Experiences.* Charlottesville, VA: Hampton Roads, 2007.

Brady, Evelyn McLean, editor. *Peaceprints: Sister Karen's Path to Nonviolence.* Buffalo, NY: Buffalo Heritage Unlimited, 2008.

Bolen, Jean Shinoda. *Close to the Bone: Life-Threatening Illness and the Search for Meaning.* New York: Scribner, 1996.

Colgrove, Melba, Harold H. Bloomfield, and Peter McWilliams, *How To Survive the Loss of a Love.* Toronto: Bantam, 1976

Doka, Ph.D., Kenneth J. *Living with Grief after Sudden Loss: Suicide, Homicide, Accident, Heart Attack, Stroke.* Washington, DC: Hospice Foundation of America, 1996.

Elmer, Lon. *Why Her Why Now: A Man's Journey through Love and Death and Grief.* Seattle: Signal Elm Press, 1987.

Feifel, Herman, Editor. *The Meaning of Death.* New York: McGraw-Hill, 1959.

Fox, Matthew. *One River, Many Wells: Wisdom Springing from Global Faiths.* New York: Tarcher/Putnam, 2000.

Frigo, Victoria, Diane Fisher and Mary Lou Cook. *You Can Help Someone Who's Grieving: A How-To Healing Handbook.* New York: Penguin, 1996.

Gawande, Atul. *Medicine and What Matters in the End.* New York: Metropolitan Books Henry Holt and Company, 2014.

Gordon, James S., and Sharon Curtin. *Comprehensive Cancer Care: Integrating Alternative, Complementary, and Conventional Therapies.* Cambridge, Massachusetts: Perseus, 2000.

Halifax, Joan. *Being With Dying: Cultivating Compassion and Fearlessness in the Presence of Death.* Boston: Shambhala, 2009.

Hine, Virginia. *Last Letter to the Pebble People.* Santa Cruz: Unity Press, 1977.

*Holy Bible.* New Revised Standard Version. Grand Rapids, Michigan: Word, 1989.

Horowitz, Karen E., and Douglas M. Lanes. *Witness To Illness: Strategies for Caregiving and Coping.* Reading, Massachusetts: Addison-Wesley, 1992.

James, John W., and Frank Cherry. *The Grief Recovery Handbook: A Step-by-Step Program for Moving Beyond Loss.* New York: Harper & Row, 1988.

Jewett, Claudia L. *Helping Children Cope with Separation and Loss.* Harvard: Harvard Common Press, 1982.

Johnson, Christopher Jay and Marsha G. McGee. *How Different Religions View Death and Afterlife.* Philadelphia: Charles Press, 1998.

Johnson, Elizabeth. *As Someone Dies: A Handbook for the Living.* Santa Monica, CA: Hay House, 1985.

Kessler, David. *The Needs of the Dying: A Guide for Bringing Hope, Comfort, and Love to Life's Final Chapter.* New York: HarperCollins, 2007

Kubler-Ross, Elisabeth. *Death: The Final Stage of Growth.* Englewood Cliffs, New Jersey: Prentice-Hall, 1975.

_____. *On Children and Death.* New York: Collier Macmillan, 1983.

_____. *On Death and Dying.* New York: Macmillan, 1969.

_____. *Questions and Answers on Death and Dying.* New York: Collier Macmillan, 1974.

LeShan, Eda. *Learning to Say Good-bye: When a Parent Dies.* New York: Avon, 1976.

Levine, Stephen. *Healing Into Life and Death.* Garden City, New York: Anchor Press/Doubleday, 1987.

_____. *Who Dies? An Investigation of Conscious Living and Conscious Dying.* Garden City, New York: Anchor Press/Doubleday, 1982.

Levine, Stephen and Ondrea. *A Year to Live: How to Live This Year as If It Were Your Last.* New York: Harmony, 1997.

Lesser, Elizabeth. *The Seeker's Guide: Making Your Life a Spiritual Adventure.* New York: Villard, 1999.

Levoy, Gregg. *Callings: Finding and Following an Authentic Life.* New York: Three Rivers Press, 1997.

Moody, Raymond A., Jr., *Life after Life*. New York: Bantam, 1975.

Muller, Wayne. *How, Then, Shall We Live? Four Simple Questions That Reveal the Beauty and Meaning of Our Lives*. New York: Bantam, 1996.

Nearing, Helen. *Loving and Leaving the Good Life*. Post Mills, Vermont: Chelsea Green Publishing, 1992.

Nuland, Sherwin B. *How We Die: Reflections on Life's Final Chapter*. New York: Alfred A. Knopf, 1993.

Remen, Rachel Naomi. *My Grandfather's Blessings: Stories of Strength*. New York: Riverhead Books, 2000.

Rinpoche, Sogyal. *The Tibetan Book of Living and Dying*. New York: HarperCollins, 1993.

Rupp, Joyce. *Fly While You Still Have Wings*. Notre Dame, Indiana: Sorin Books, 2015.

Sattilaro, Anthony J. *Recalled By Life*. New York: Avon, 1982.

Shakespeare, William. *The Complete Works*. Baltimore, Maryland: Penguin Books, 1969.

Siegel, Bernie S. *Love, Medicine and Miracles*. New York: Harper & Row, 1968.

_____. *Peace, Love and Healing: Bodymind Communication & the Path to Self-healing: An Exploration*. New York: Harper & Row, 1989.

Sikking, Robert P. *A Matter of Life and Death.* Marina del Ray, CA: DeVorss, 1978.

Simonton, O. Carl, Stephanie Matthews-Simonton, and James L. Creighton. *Getting Well Again: A Step-by-Step, Self-Help Guide to Overcoming Cancer for Patients and Their Families.* Toronto: Bantam, 1978.

Singh, Kathleen Dowling. *The Grace In Aging: Awaken As You Grow Older.* Boston: Wisdom, 2014.

Tick, Edward. *War and the Soul: Healing Our Nation's Veterans from Post-traumatic Stress Disorder.* Wheaton, Illinois: Quest Books, 2005.

Varley, Susan. *Badger's Parting Gifts.* New York: Lathrop, Lee & Shephard Books, 1984.

# Index

www.PatriciaGulinoLansky.com

Made in the USA
Middletown, DE
06 March 2016